OPEN COCKPIT

OPEN COCKPIT

A Pilot of the Royal Flying Corps

Arthur Gould Lee
Air Vice-Marshal, Royal Air Force

Grub Street • London

Published by
Grub Street
4 Rainham Close
London SW11 6SS

Reprinted 2013

First published 1969 by Jarrolds Publishers (London) Ltd
© Arthur Gould Lee 1969
This edition first published 2012
© Grub Street 2012

British Library Cataloguing in Publication Data

Lee, Arthur Stanley Gould.
  Open cockpit.
  1. Lee, Arthur Stanley Gould. 2. World War, 1914-1918--
  Aerial operations, British. 3. World War, 1914-1918--
  Personal narratives, British.
  I. Title
  940.4'4941'092-dc23

ISBN-13: 9781908117250

Cover design and book formatting by Sarah Driver

Printed and bound in Great Britain by Berforts Group, UK
Grub Street Publishing only uses FSC (Forest Stewardship Council) paper for its
books.

THE PUBLISHER WOULD PARTICULARLY LIKE TO THANK ANTHONY SAVELL
AND SAM GOWER FOR THEIR HELP IN BRINGING THIS PUBLICATION TO FRUITION.

CONTENTS

To David
my grandson
a subaltern of the Blues and Royals and a fledgling flyer too

One crowded hour of glorious life
Is worth an age without a name
Thomas O. Mordaunt 1791

AUTHOR'S NOTE

In my book *No Parachute* I described eight months' flying in France on Sopwith Pups and Camels with No. 46 Fighter Squadron, Royal Flying Corps, from May 1917 to January 1918. *Open Cockpit* covers a longer period, from the time I learned to fly in 1916 until, my active service spell completed, I taught others to fly Camels up to and just after the end of the war.

The aeroplanes which I flew, additional to Pups and Camels, included the Maurice Farman and Avro on which I did my initial flying training, and the range of B.E.s on which I carried out the first phase of my so-called advanced training. All these machines were, by modern standards, about as primitive as bows and arrows. Not only were they fragile in construction—wooden, wire-braced frameworks and wings, covered with doped fabric—but rudimentary in their layout and equipment.

Every aeroplane of the day had an open cockpit in which one sat swathed in layers of woollen underclothing, fleece-lined leather great-coats and sheepskin thigh-boots, with which to resist the petrifying cold three or four miles up. There was no heating, no oxygen for high flying, no retractable undercarriage, no engine starter, no radio links with air or ground, no brakes to help with landing and taxi-ing, and, most vital of all, no parachutes. And there were no instruments worth the name. But we did carry a hammer to correct

1

simple machine-gun stoppages!

Open Cockpit tells how the fighter pilots of the First World War flew and fought and instructed on these elementary early planes. So far as the chapters on combat flying are concerned, I have drawn on descriptions written on the spot at the time, mostly in letters. The sections on learning to fly, and on teaching others to fly, are recollections prompted largely by the entries in my flying log-books and other contemporary records.

Grateful acknowledgements are rendered to the following: Mr Gerald Austin of Jarrolds for his helpful promptings and suggestions during the planning of this book; Group Captain Guy M. Knocker for reawakening dormant memories of Joyce Green; and Mrs Frank R. Senn, of Florida, U.S.A., for alerting me to the active interest taken today in the United States in First World War aviation, and particularly in the knightly figure of Manfred von Richtofen.

I wish also to express my deep thanks to the following for their valuable assistance in providing me with some of the more notable photographs in this book: John Harris, G. Denham Jenkins, M. P. Marsh, H. A. Oxley, Alex Revell, L. A. Rogers, D. J. Stephens and W. J. (Jack) Wales; and particularly W. J. (Bill) Evans and Alex Imrie for their rare selection of 'in flight' pictures of German World War I aircraft, and H. G. W. Debenham (the only flyer to serve in 46 Squadron first as an observer and later as a pilot) for his equally rare pictures of British 1917 aeroplanes in flight, with especial mention of the probably unique shot of a Nieuport under archie fire. I should add that to the best of my knowledge, these 'in flight' photographs, as well as the majority of the others, have never been published previously.

Acknowledgement is also paid to the following publications which have been consulted for factual detail: *The War in the Air*, Vols iii and iv, by H. A. Jones, *Sixty Squadron, R.A.F.*, by Group Captain A.J.L. Scott, C.B., M.C., A.F.E., and three of the Harleyford Publications. *Air Aces of the 1914–18 War, Fighter Aircraft of the 1914–18 War*, and *Richtofen and the Flying Circus*.

A.G.L.
1969

FOREWORD

I brought the car to a halt, for I recognised the brick-built shrine, half smothered in ivy, that stood at the side of the track leading to Beaupré Farm, and to the encampment that had clustered by it during most of the First World War. The shrine, with its protecting glass-panelled doors, was a little dilapidated now, but someone had placed fresh flowers in a jar before the figure of the Virgin Mary.

Ahead of us should have been the line of canvas hangars backing on to the cobbled road that ran between La Gorgue and the larger town of Merville to the west, but they were no longer there. And the fields stretching north to the River Lys, that had once been our aerodrome, were now a vast plain of corn. In the burning July afternoon the heat shimmered over the flat expanse in quivering waves, just as it had done years before, in 1917, when I was young and a fledgling fighter pilot.

I turned the car off the road, and drove slowly towards the farm, a customary, one-story quadrilateral centred by a midden. The farm was exactly as I had known it in the past, even to the smell of the midden, but the wooden hutments had gone, save for a few of the largest, among them the long black-painted shed that had been the Officers' Mess, and a smaller one which I had shared with three other pilots.

Nobody came from the farm to ask our business, for everyone was at work in the fields. Fifty yards in front of us was the line of poplars

3

along the banks of the River Lys, or, as we usually called it, the canal, for such in fact it was, giving passage to giant barges, some under their own steam, some towed by horses on the towpath.

I left the car and walked to the bank of the river. And as I stood there, gazing at its turbid waters flowing sluggishly westwards, just as they had always done, nostalgia suddenly flooded over me. I closed my eyes, and out of the mists of time came voices long since stilled. I heard shouts and laughter, and the splashing of swimmers and divers, sounds that echoed here so many years ago. I heard again the voices of those who were to die within the year, sometimes of youngsters who frolicked in these waters only a few hours before they met their fate in the air.

A verse of Swinburne's that had laid dormant in my mind since boyhood came unerringly to me now.

> That no life lives for ever;
>> That dead men rise up never;
> That even the weariest river
>> Winds somewhere safe to sea.

Down the long shafts of memory I saw them, my comrades of decades ago, romping in the water, having fun with home-made boats and rafts. I heard again the yells and the guffaws as they ducked each other, saw them clambering up the bank, wrapping themselves in towels, strolling to the Mess, sitting casually in the baking summer sun, smoking, chatting, reading. Maybe within the hour they would be on their way to the hangars at the other side of the aerodrome, there to climb into their waiting aeroplanes and go aloft on patrol. Maybe an hour earlier they had descended from frenzied battle in the skies, and having made their reports in the sweltering squadron office, had rushed over to the Mess, and within minutes were in the cooling river.

I went back to the two sheds that had survived. The Mess, where we had eaten and indulged in our riotous binges, now had its windows battened, but through a half-open door I saw piles of produce and farming implements. My own hut, with one end opened up, was a shelter for a couple of tractors. The wooden floor had gone, and chickens scratched busily in the corner where my bed had stood. But in my memory it was my batman Watt that I saw, standing by the bed, roping into a tidy bundle the valise and clothes of that morning's fatal casualty. 'Such a nice gentleman, he was, sir,' came his voice dolefully through the years.

Because during these few minutes time stood still, I saw them all again as I returned to the Mess, standing around the entrance, awaiting the call to dinner—Courtneidge and Asher, Odell and Barrager, Kay and McDonald, Joske and Wilcox and all the rest. Most of them were younger than me, and I was but twenty-two. They lived under the daily summons of death, but they were light of heart, high in spirit. There was badinage and mirth, especially when Marchant and Dimmock began their clowning. I heard Marchant's stentorian 'Put that cow down, Murgatroyd!' then the burst of laughter, the call for another round of drinks, and soon the trooping indoors to eat.

I remembered how sometimes after dinner, when the mood took us, we resumed our drinks around the piano while bellowing bawdy doggerel. And some of the carefree songs we chorused those years ago still echoed in the air. 'So Early in the Morning, Before the Break of Day' and 'Dirty Danny's digging deeper dugouts' and 'The only only way, the only trick to play' and half a dozen others. How readily they came back with all the other ghosts!

It was a rare existence that we led, with its sharp contrast between comfort and good cheer on the ground and deadly hazard among the clouds, but we did not reflect often on it. We lived for the day, for the hour. We lived for the adventure, for the excitement of fighting in the skies. After all, that was what most of us had volunteered for.

And as I stood there on ground that had known all our footsteps, I realised that of the four aerodromes on which I served in France, La Gorgue, Bruay, St Marie Capelle and Izel le Hameau, it was La Gorgue which had stayed most nostalgically in the memory. Not even Izel, that paradise of a wartime billet set in the orchard of

Filescamp Farm, the orchard that knew the heroic spirit of Ball, Bishop and MacLaren and dozens of other stalwarts, and that boasted such famous sanctums as the Abode of Love—not even the rich associations of Izel could deprive La Gorgue of its unique distinction.

For at La Gorgue I was introduced to war. It was here that I stepped unreadily into the first thrilling chapter of my young life. Here I plunged headlong into excitements and emotions that I had never encountered before and was never to experience again with such stark intensity. For only when you are young can you relish to the full the exhilarating sensations of mortal danger.

Never afterwards was I to feel those first shattering impacts of seeing men killed, and of killing them myself, and of escaping the same fate, again and again, by the most unholy luck. Never afterwards was I to recapture entirely the pulse-quickening openings of those first encounters with enemy aeroplanes miles above the earth. Nor the first tense pressures of the joystick trigger to shoot a twisting Albatros a hundred yards from me. Nor those heart-stopping moments in my first breathless dog-fights when tracers streaked past my head and I dazedly realised that death had missed me by inches.

But when happenings such as these, repeated many times during the weeks and months, became almost routine they no longer held their original exaltation. The first flush of the flame of air fighting had died down. Our numbers thinned, the faces in the Mess changed, I became a hardened survivor. I was much older, not in years but in sense and experience, for character quickly matured in the Royal Flying Corps. Yet though I changed, La Gorgue remained as fresh as ever, the place where I had come as an ignorant fledgling, the scene of my initiation into a ruthless frightening but ultimately splendid way of life and death.

Above all, it was at La Gorgue that I first entered into the tight, self-contained community of a squadron of fighter pilots, a miniature cosmos drawn from every corner of the Empire, whose occupants had little interest in anything but the job of mounting into the blue on a fragile aeroplane with the one object of killing or being killed.

Yet the daily risk of a violent end was accepted unconcernedly. It was something we never spoke of and seldom consciously thought about. But for me it bred a hitherto unknown bond with other men—comradeship forged in the heat of dangers repeatedly shared. How remarkable was the understanding we found in each other, the camaraderie on the ground, and the unity and trust during our deadly combats in the skies. Yet most of us had never met until a few weeks, or even days, before.

It was the recollection of these brief fellowships that had so suddenly enveloped me by the River Lys. And now, standing by Beaupré Farm, surrounded still by the shades of the past, I looked across the once broad aerodrome to the hangars no longer there, and my thoughts went to those distant days when, in the company of the flyers of La Gorgue, and of the others who followed them, I embarked upon the great adventure of fighting in the air.

ONE
FLYING START

'We're on the N.O.P.,' said the acting 'A' Flight commander, Mc-Donald, who was leading our formation of six. 'As some of you new chaps haven't flown with me before, I'll run through the signals.'

He meant Courtneidge, Odell and me, all from 'C' Flight. Normally we flew only with members of our own flights, but because of casualties and Headquarters demands for more and bigger patrols, the flight commanders had to draw on each others' pilots to spread the work out evenly. By N.O.P., McDonald was referring to North Offensive Patrol, which covered the northern half of 46 Squadron's front from Lens nearly to Dixmude, north of Ypres. The S.O.P. covered the southern half. There were also the Line Patrol and the Close Offensive Patrol, which to me were identical. In fact, so far as my brief experience went, all patrols worked out in practice to be more or less the same, except the D.O.P., the Distant Offensive, but no doubt these fastidious distinctions kept staff officers busy and happy parcelling out our jobs in tidy twenty-mile beats.

'Of course, you know that when I rock my wings,' went on Mc-Donald, 'I've spotted Huns and I'm going to attack. If you see a Hun before me, dive in front and rock your wings and point to where he is, then get back into position damn quick. If your engine goes dud, dive in front and switchback, then go home. The same with a gun jam you can't correct. Now for Very light signals. White for washout, red for rally or enemy seen, green for distress. But don't use them unless you really have to—they give our position away to all and sundry. All clear?'

We nodded, as we continued putting on our flying gear, standing in 'A' Flight hangar.

'If we attack, don't fire until I do. That's important. And pull out to the flanks clear of me before you press the trigger. That's for two-seaters. If we meet a formation, or if we're bounced, well, after the first scrimmage, it's every man for himself. And keep a sharp look-out—we may run into the bloody Baron's Flying Circus again.'

That morning, he and Wilcox had been in a formation of nine, led by the 'B' Flight commander, which encountered Baron von Richtofen's formidable Jasta, and engaged in a series of dog-fights, in which neither side managed a certain kill, but, as usual, the Pups couldn't match the performance of the Albatros D–IIIs, and our pilots were both skilful and lucky to emerge with whole skins. Wilcox especially was badly shot about, and with his controls cut, had crashed heavily on landing, yet here he was on patrol again, and, like the rest of us, fully expecting another meeting with the Circus.

'No need to come too close in formation,' McDonald continued as he led the way out of the hangar, 'and if archie gets too attentive, don't disperse, just stay in position and follow my jinking.'

I listened closely to all he said, in case he told me something new. For us fledglings there were so many things to learn, and so little time to learn them. It was seldom that a flight commander or patrol leader thought to give us the benefit of his experience by passing on a few useful tips, and we had to find things out for ourselves—and if we failed to find out, we didn't last long. My education had begun with some sharp lessons soon after I arrived in the squadron, and it was then that I discovered that almost all the theory of air fighting that I'd been taught in England was valueless compared with experience.

I'd been in 46 Squadron nearly a fortnight and although in the course of ten patrols I'd got over the feeling of being a new boy slightly looked down upon by the oldsters, a couple of chastening clashes with Albatros fighters had made me realise that in this business of air fighting I was still a complete beginner. Yet two of the pilots on this patrol, Odell and Wilcox, were greener even than me, though like me they were learning fast.

McDonald was already climbing into his machine as we 'C' Flight pilots walked along the tarmac to our planes. I stepped up into mine, Sopwith Scout A 6202, fastened my safety-belt to preclude being thrown out in a dog-fight, then went through the usual routine. First I checked round the cockpit to make sure that the 2½ lb hammer, for rectifying gun-jams, was in its leather socket, as well as the Colt automatic pistol, the fire extinguisher, the Very pistol and cartridges, plus the slab of chocolate (one got peckish on long patrols), the prisoner-of-war haversack (shaving gear, toothbrush, socks, shoes and so on) and the handkerchief in the pocket across the breast of the flying coat—the chilly air high up was inducive to dribbling! And of course I was well enveloped in flying clothing, for although we were only going to 15,000 feet, I had learned that even at this height I could become excessively cold sitting in an open cockpit for a couple of hours or more.

Then a quick look at the instruments. Watch wound up? Correct? The compass moving freely? Height indicator set at zero? Bubble centred in the curved lateral-angle indicator? Both map-boards (folding north-south strips, one for line, the other for distant, patrols) in their flaps? Was the mirror clean?—a small, circular reflector fixed to the rear starboard centre-section strut, and quite useless for its alleged purpose of spotting Huns coming up from behind. And last, but far from least, was the Aldis gunsight lens free from smears of castor oil?

These all checked, I am ready to start the engine, and I nod to the fitter waiting in front of the machine. He at once calls out 'Switch off', which I repeat, then 'Petrol on' and 'Suck in', both of which I repeat. He swings the propeller round four or five times, and stands back, while I adjust the petrol-air mixture.

'Contact, sir.'

I repeat 'Contact' and press the switch. He heaves the propeller down with a strong pull, stepping clear in the same movement. The willing Le Rhône engine starts immediately, and as the fitter had warmed it up ten minutes previously, I am able, after ensuring that an ack-emma, otherwise air mechanic, is lying across the fuselage near the tail, to test without delay at full throttle. As I check the rev counter, the plane throbs and sways under the pull of the rotating engine and propeller, and strains to move forward, but is held by the chocks and the men at the wing-tips. Then I throttle down and load the Vickers gun by pressing the lever under the fairing just in front of me. I still get a kick out of doing this, for it sets the seal on my being in the war—I'm going up not just to fly but to fight.

I wave my gloved hand, the mechanics draw away the chocks, and I taxi briskly along the tarmac after Courtneidge, the two airmen holding on to the wing-tips. We follow McDonald along a narrow track flanked by root crops to a cindered area in the middle of the farmland. After Courtneidge takes off, I wheel into position to go next. The senior mechanic searches the air to make sure that no machine is about to land, and salutes to indicate 'All clear!' I pull down my goggles, wave my gauntleted hand once more, the men let go the wing-tips, I open the throttle wide, the Pup moves forward, gathers speed, the tail comes up, the crops whizz by. A short succession of wheel trundlings and bumps, then we're off, climbing steeply to clear the poplar trees at the side of the aerodrome. I join the patrol leader, who is circling slowly at 1,000 feet, and when everyone is in formation, off we go, towards the war, three miles up.

I was still sufficiently a beginner to feel a thrill of pride whenever I mounted into the air to go on patrol, for each flight reminded me that I was part of this fabulous enterprise of seeking out an enemy to do battle among the clouds. And there was ample time to reflect on such romantic notions as we climbed steadily in two V–sections of three, with Williams and Wilcox behind McDonald, and Odell and me behind Courtneidge, who kept us in echelon to the right about two hundred feet behind and above McDonald's section. Odell and I were thus landed with the main responsibility for guarding the tails of the whole group, and this meant that once across the Lines we had to turn our heads every two or three minutes to scan the skies astern.

McDonald, as leader, flew a red streamer from each rear strut, and Courtneidge, as deputy, one from his rudder. Tyro though I was, I had already flown the deputy-leader streamer when Courtneidge, two days earlier, led Odell and me on a Line Patrol, and was much elated when I saw my rigger attaching the red strip to the rudder. I could hardly believe it after only a week. But advancement could be quick in a scout squadron in France.

The day was fine, with blue sky and scattered arrays of white-topped cumulus rising to about 8,000 feet. As we lifted higher, horizontal visibility was low on account of the dense heat haze, but at 3,000 we abruptly mounted above it, and looked down on its shining level surface, like a lake of quicksilver. Ascending still higher, we could see vertically through it. Hovering well above its mirror surface was the string of observation balloons, set a few miles apart some four or five miles from the trenches. They floated there motionless, like comatose hippos, seeming both pathetic and ludicrous, although the observer's job was far from that, with only his parachute to save him when Hun fighters set his gas-bag alight.

As we approached the Ypres salient, I saw several of our two-seaters, B.E.s and R.E.8s, doing their shoots, seemingly stationary as usual, and above them formations of Spads and Nieuports and also a group of the new S.E.5s. They were all concentrated in the N.O.P. area, as they have been for the past week, and none of us understood why. Not until a day or so later were we to learn that our task was to prevent the German reconnaissance and photographic and artillery-spotting aircraft discovering that we were about to launch the Battle of Messines.

But to keep so many aeroplanes patrolling the skies at all heights throughout daylight hours had meant that we, like every other squadron, had to work hard, usually two and sometimes three patrols a day. These were meant to last two hours at patrol height, but as we took around half an hour to reach the higher levels, and about twenty minutes to descend gradually, they averaged nearly three hours. German fighters seldom beat up and down the front in the way that we did, but raided us in strength when they chose, as Richtofen's squadron had done in the morning, and they invariably intercepted and mauled our weaker formations.

From 6,000 feet I surveyed the Lines as we flew north, though as yet still to their westwards, and so secure from attack. Strange how accustomed we were not to expect to meet German fighters on our side of the Lines, but they had no need to come, for profiting from our unvarying offensive policy, they found all the British planes they could handle either above the trenches or well into their territory.

I gazed down upon the broad band of shell-pitted front lines, looking like the surface of the moon, which emerged from the haze that masked everything north of Ypres and sprawled under us towards the east of Armentières until it disappeared into the southern horizon. Open for us to inspect were all the secrets of this waste of tortured soil that wound across Belgium and France, a barrier along which millions of armed men crouched in foul trenches, facing each other behind barbed wire, like animals in zoos. Below us lay displayed the zigzagging entrenchments, the wriggling communications to the rear, the untidy belts of rusty wire in no-man's-land—all the cunningly contrived warrens of trench warfare, which us flyers could examine not only with detachment but with gratitude that we were not there, too.

We passed over this tragic evidence of the incredible stupidity of mankind, and climbed steadily into Hunland. I still had a curious feeling of trespassing every time I flew across this invisible wall rising to infinity above the Lines, in fact I would not have been unduly staggered had a squad of airborne German policemen magically appeared and peremptorily ordered us to keep out!

As we rose higher and higher, I intently searched the now clouding skies to the eastwards, but could discern no threatening specks to worry about. I suddenly shivered, and a glance at the altimeter showed that we were at 15,000 feet. Now we were well into Hunland, which from this height was but a vast pattern of green woods and brown fields, with straight white roads cutting through, and others winding between, like lacework. Here and there were the dark splodges of big towns, with tails of smoke trailing north-eastwards under the prevailing wind. But still no sign of enemy fighters. What had happened to the Bad Baron and his Circus of gaily painted Albatroses?

All the way up, the six of us had scarcely changed position in relation to each other. We seemed to hang inertly in the air, tied together by unseen threads, enveloped in the unbroken thunder of our engines. But suddenly the crack of machine-gun fire broke the spell. By now I knew the sound, not the harsh crash of twin German Spandaus but McDonald testing his Vickers. I saw the tracers flashing eastwards. The rest of us tested our guns too, then swung back to our positions.

I looked towards Courtneidge, on my left front. He sat perfectly still, slightly bent forward, peering past his tiny windscreen. Suddenly, as though aware that my eyes were upon him, he turned his helmeted head, and below the goggles-mask I saw his smile as he lifted his gloved hand in friendly fashion. I waved back, curiously warmed by this gesture in mid-air, three miles above the earth. He and I, and the four others, none of whom I had met before I came to La Gorgue, were now thrown willy-nilly into this aerial fraternity, for no purpose but to fight German flyers to the death.

We now began the patrol, north and south, some five miles over the Lines. For once we were not harried by archie, for he had so many targets lower down that he couldn't be bothered to shoot at us at 15,000, and so we sailed along unmolested, still speculating on where this morning's Huns had gone. And with nothing much to think about I got to wondering why we call them Huns. Hardly because of the barbarous manner of the German invasion of Belgium and France, for this did not explain why flying instructors at training schools in England derisively dubbed their pupils Huns. Nor did it explain why, in France, we called not only our airborne enemies, but also their planes, by the same mocking epithet. There seemed no rational answer to the question.

We pursued our beat up and down at three-quarters throttle, and with each uneventful run the patrol dragged the more, each course seeming to take an interminable time. Turning north once again, I glanced at the dashboard watch as we passed over Lille, and noted 4.30, then while we flew towards our northern turning point, Roulers, resolutely kept my eyes off the watch until we got there, imagining as we swung round that it must surely now be five o'clock. But the watch said 4.45. Impossible, I thought, angrily, it must have stopped. But it hadn't, and this waiting-for-the-kettle-to-boil would go on for two hours—unless we ran into Huns.

My mind-wandering soon ceases. We have been up over an hour, are still at 15,000, ten miles or more into Hunland, and have found nobody to fight. The weather is gradually changing, for the banks of cumulus are closing together, the atmosphere is not so clear, and we see less of the ground as McDonald swings us between vast masses of cloud. Suddenly he veers to the left and dips a little. Has he seen an E.A.? I search downwards but can see nothing. Then half a minute later, as we approach Roulers, he rocks his wings and drops into a dive. We follow. I stare at the motley countryside below and can't spot what he is after, but Courtneidge does, and draws us off to the flank, to give room to fire.

The dive steepens, and I still peer ahead, baffled. Then suddenly two aeroplanes take shape against the mosaic of fields and woods— two-seaters, flying north, side by side, coming towards us, both camouflaged in a kind of dappled brown. No wonder they were hard to see! Now that I have found them, and we are attacking, my heart begins to quicken with excitement. We are still over 2,000 feet above them, too far away to fire, and they haven't seen us yet because we are approaching them head-on.

With gentle touches of the joystick and rudder-bar, I aim my machine until the right-hand Hun centres the ring of the Aldis sight, and as I keep it there, waiting for McDonald to open fire, it grows larger every second. My right eye is glued to the sight, my fingers tighten on the joystick handle, thumb ready to press the Bowden grip that controls the trigger of the Vickers.

At 300 hundred yards McDonald's tracer flashes away, and my thumb gently presses the little lever. A second later six lines of smoking white tracer are converging on the quarry. At once, the two Huns swing east, and from the front of each comes a plume of black smoke. For an instant I have the incredible hope that they are both on fire, but then I remember—they are L.V.G.s that have opened up their engines in a hurry, and the greasy smoke is pouring for a few seconds from the chimney-like exhausts that rise up from the engine and discharge rearwards over the top of the centre section.

We dive towards them, engines full on, in an ever-steepening angle. The Pup shudders, the wires scream even above the roar of the Le Rhône. I am quivering with the thrill of it, but I aim through the Aldis very carefully, firing bursts of about twenty rounds. I can't understand why we don't hit them, especially as we are gaining on them under the impetus of our dive. As they pass by the flank of a cloud, their back guns blaze up at us defiantly, swinging from one to the other of us in turn. I see a few tracers coming up at me, but they are off target, and I don't even hear them.

I draw sufficiently close to see the white edging to the Iron Crosses on the top wings, and to note the yellow-brown of the observer's coat, but that is as near as we get, for they begin to dive, and draw away. Once more aiming dead-on, I press the trigger and after five shots—silence! The hellish, startling shock of silence. My gun has jammed! I seize the hammer from its socket alongside my right leg, and still in the dive, give the cocking handle a sharp crack. The handle falls, and as I steer and fire with my left hand, my right goes to replace the hammer, but in my eagerness, I miss the socket, and the hammer falls to the fabric floor of the cockpit.

I continue firing, then again comes blank silence. Another jam! The hammer lies on the floor, beyond my reach—and I can't correct the stoppage without it. I level out, and in a flash the formation disappears beneath me. I sit there cursing, cursing my carelessness, cursing the gun, cursing the dud ammunition, cursing the squadron gunnery officer whose job it is to see that we don't have these damned failures. I look round. It seems an age since McDonald opened fire, but it was little more than a minute ago. I think, What the hell do I do now? I've got to get the hammer somehow, or else go home. And I'm not going to do that. I unfasten my safety-belt and reach down, stretching vainly, for my searching fingers can't get there.

I pull my feet from the rudder-bar straps, twist as far down and side-ways in the seat as the narrow cockpit allows. I touch the hammer with the tips of my fingers. More twisting and wriggling side-ways, with my head below the fairing, while the uncontrolled Pup rises, stalls and falls over in a spin. But at last my fingers get under the handle—a second later I've got the hammer!

I work myself back into my seat, bring the Pup to her senses and hit the cocking handle. It won't move. Several more hard cracks. Still it doesn't fall. I am sweating like a pig, panting all out, cursing in-sanely. A frantic succession of fierce blows. The bloody cartridge just won't go in the breech.

I force myself to calm down, then standing up, and holding the joystick with my left hand, I hit the cocking handle half a dozen times with all the force I can muster. Suddenly the obstinate round goes in. I press the trigger, the Vickers cracks away reassuringly. I sit down, carefully replace the hammer, fasten my belt, get my feet back in the holding straps, and again look around me.

My formation has long since vanished and I am alone. Although I know I must be at least ten miles over, I haven't the faintest notion where I am, for there is nothing below I can recognise, nothing but open countryside. My height is 9,000 feet, and there is no sense in staying around at this, for a Pup, highly dangerous level hoping to run into the patrol again. It is not a truly happy situation for an in-experienced pilot, but at least I'm not a complete greenhorn.

Then just as I realised by the position of the sun, quickly con-firmed by the compass, that I was flying eastwards, I saw ahead, stand-ing out plainly against a wall of grey cloud, three planes approaching from Hunland, and higher than me by 300 feet. They spotted me and came down in a sudden steep curve. They were silhouetted clearly against the blue sky above. V-strutters! Albatroses!

I was petrified with fright, and my first instinct was to dive down with full engine, and a week ago I would have done so. But I didn't, for now I knew that this was the fatal thing to do, because they could dive much faster than me. I started to circle slowly, waiting for the first shots, shaking with wind-up, knowing that even though I was staying to fight it out, I was almost certainly a goner. I was watching for the first tracer, ready to kick the rudder, to skid clear. But they held their fire, and the suspense was making me feel sick in the stomach. Why weren't they firing? I gazed at them fascinated as they came even lower, and banked steeply.

Then unbelievingly I saw the roundels on their wings. They weren't D–IIIs at all, but Nieuport Scouts, which are V-strutters too. I sank back in my seat, benumbed with relief. I thought, Thank God I didn't dive away—what a fool I'd have looked! But what a fool not to recognise them. It was because they'd come from the east, and, anyway, I wasn't the first to confuse them with Albatroses. It happened often with beginners. And it sometimes happened that an unwary pilot found a supposed Nieuport trying to shoot him down.

I waved to them and they waved back, then as they resumed formation, I took up position behind. They were flying south-west, obviously making for home—and me with them! Then came reaction, and I lifted my head and roared with laughter until the tears rolled down under my goggles. I even hoped that a bunch of Huns would come along, so that I could have a scrap in good company, but all we saw were some Sopwith 1½-strutters being archied. We were archied too, but only four salvos, and not too accurate—the Nieuport leader didn't even jink. As we reached the Lines, and they started to lose height southwards, I drew ahead and waved cheerio, and saw them wave in return. They were, I supposed, from No 1 Squadron, going down to their aerodrome at Bailleul.

But I still had over half an hour's patrol to do, and I decided to try to join a Line Patrol. I was now at 7,000, much too low for a Pup, and I climbed northwards to 13,000, where I ran into a formation of five S.E.5s, but when I attempted to ease into position behind them, I found that they flew as fast as Albatroses, and soon left me behind.

I then went further north and had a look at the flooded lands in the Dixmude area, where the Belgians had broken the dykes and put miles of low-lying countryside under water to hinder the German advance to the coast. Returning south, at 15,000, I spotted two Spads to the east of me. They are French made and look Hunnish, so I approached cautiously, then, reassured, closed up behind them. Five minutes later they began a dive on a Hun two-seater well beyond Houthulst Forest, north of Ypres. I dived with them, and fired when they did, and got off fifty rounds when once more the Vickers jammed. Both the Spads and the Hun, also diving, were much too fast for me, and for the second time I lost a patrol while getting the gun going.

Feeling much deflated, I continued beating up and down between Polygon Wood, east of Ypres and Ploegsteert Wood, meeting a patrol of Naval triplanes and another of F.E.8s from 41 Squadron, but never McDonald and the Pups, and as nobody seemed to want me I carried on by myself. No doubt futile, but it gave me a good feeling to pilot my frail cockleshell on my solitary own, miles above the earthbound armies in those ugly brown trenches below.

Eventually I noted that I'd been up over the two hours, and descended in a slow corkscrew over Ypres, down almost to ground level. I circled the poor, battered city, and had a close look at the moated citadel walls, then went back to La Gorgue, never higher than a hundred feet, a thrilling ride over a countryside littered with scores of army camps and depots.

McDonald and the others were already back, having had no luck with the L.V.G.s we'd chased, nor with another two-seater encountered later. The heat was stifling, and we hurriedly threw aside our flying gear, then, after putting in our reports, drove to the Mess in a Crossley tender, and lost no time in plunging thankfully into the River Lys. All the pilots off duty were already in the water, except the few who, amazingly, could fly but not swim! We watched a patrol come in, and within a quarter of an hour the pilots were in the water too. They'd had two fights, and shot down an Albatros, seen to crash near Comines.

Those hot June days and lazy hours by the river were the heights of bliss, and war seemed far away, even though we'd been in it an hour before. Looking back over the afternoon's show, I realised that I'd enjoyed it, particularly my fledgling, one-man patrol, and I found myself thinking, with some surprise, Well, I suppose this *can* be a lovely war at times! Certainly today came up to all the ardent expectations with which I'd started to learn to fly nearly twelve months before.

TWO

FLEDGLING FLASHBACK

Of course, it was a fool thing to want to do, because I'd barely learned to fly, and, as I was soon to realise, knew next to nothing about real piloting. But the impulse had come, on the spur of a clear, calm February morning, and the knowledge that I might not have another chance.

After circling Filton aerodrome in my new single-seater B.E.12 scout, which I naïvely imagined to be the hottest plane in the Royal Flying Corps, I had turned idly towards the Avon, at about 1,000 feet, and as I gazed at the river winding towards Bristol, I suddenly realised that this was just the moment to fulfil the secret ambition that would set the seal on my having learned to be a pilot—nothing less than to fly under Clifton Suspension Bridge.

I had completed all the tests for graduation, and my wings should come any time now—in fact, they were granted that very day, the 10th, Central Flying School Certificate No 3095—but there was this quite unofficial test, a 'must' to every pupil of spirit at Filton, which I had to pass to prove, not to authority but to myself, that I could fly.

Throttling back, I lost height quickly. The normal clatter of the Royal Aircraft Factory engine became nearly a purr. I flew westward along the Avon towards the bridge, dropped gently down between the steep rocky sides of the gorge, which had an awkward curve at exactly the wrong place, and skimmed over a bulging wooded hill on my right. As I neared the bridge, doing all of seventy miles an hour, I saw traffic passing over, and then I was there, flying a hundred feet beneath. It was all so easy. I ventured to glance up, and saw people leaning over looking at me. I didn't worry. In those days nobody bothered to report such high spirits.

There was ample room, for the bridge was 250 feet above the water, and the effective width of the gorge was over 300 feet, but I had to be careful, as I had a little drift. Once through, I climbed up and away to the south, clear of the city, then, feeling decidedly braced, set out at 6,000 feet on a cross-country to Cardiff and Gloucester.

Though by standards acquired later, my stunt called for no great skill—Colonel McClean had flown a Short seaplane under the Tower Bridge, a much trickier needle to thread, some four years earlier—I was still in the throes of learning, and I was flying a heavy, cumbersome B.E.12. But my effort was a stepping-stone to progress. I had done something I did not have to do, which had seemed a forbidding proposition, and which had turned out to be nothing at all.

Five months (less five weeks in hospital and on sick leave) twenty hours' solo and two crashes away, I had begun the business of learning to fly with No 24 Reserve Squadron at Netheravon. On the evening of August 10th, 1916, I had my first-ever flight as passenger in a French Maurice Farman Shorthorn, which was the standard elementary trainer for the R.F.C., the purblind British Government having neglected before the war to provide for such a need. I did not touch the controls but just sat there, entranced, skimming over the vastness of Salisbury Plain at 200 feet. My instructor, a burly good-natured Canadian, Lieutenant Lascelles, gave me a twelve-minute trip to break the ice. At a time when to fly was the privilege of the very few, this first plunge into a new element, in a flimsy pusher plane, sitting at the point of a nacelle that jutted out in front of the wings like the back end of a shoe, was a wonderful, wonderful thrill. Although I didn't know it, the Maurice Farman was, in fact, only slightly in advance of the machine which the Wright brothers had first flown some ten or twelve years before.

Next morning my Initial Flying Training proper began. At seven o' clock I was one of a score of pupils sitting in a line outside the flight shed, perched on empty petrol cans. We wore an assortment of uniforms—infantry, cavalry, gunners, engineers, all in breeches and putties or field-boots, Scots in kilts, and a sprinkling of R.F.C. Special Reserve in their maternity jackets and split-ass caps (there were two four-letter words for it). We were waiting our turn to be called by our instructors: mine was already in the air.

Suddenly a figure appeared from a flank and stood before us. We stood up smartly to attention, for he was the Major. I was nearest to him. He fixed me with a hostile eye, pointed, said 'You!', and beckoned me to follow. I trotted expectantly behind as he led the way to a Rumpety, as the Farmans were always called, and gestured me to get aboard. I wormed my way through the network of flying and landing wires, stood on a tyre, and climbed into the nacelle, slung halfway between the wings. He got in the back seat, had the engines behind us started, and taxied clear of the hangars. The aerodrome stretched emptily before us.

He tapped me on the shoulder. 'Fasten your helmet, you damn fool!' he shouted, 'and drop your goggles!' I hastily obeyed. He opened up the engine, took off, climbed to 300 feet, tapped me again, and yelled 'Take her over'.

I was petrified. I had no idea what to do. I gazed at the control, a sort of cycle handlebar with looped ends, known as the spectacles, set on a central column. Below was a rudder bar for my feet. I timidly rested my hands on the loops, and let my toes gently touch the rudder. For a minute the plane kept on a straight course, then the right wing started to drop, the looped bar followed, and she began to slip side-ways. I was fascinated, waiting for something to happen.

'Straighten her up, you bloody fool!' came a bellow in my ear. Desperately, I pressed the bar down further to the right. The right wing dropped steeper, and went on dropping.

'What the f—g hell are you trying to do, you bleeding idiot?' came the bellow.

In a panic, I pushed the handlebar away from me. The Rumpety dipped her nose indignantly, shuddered, banked suddenly over. Then the controls were snatched from my feeble hands, and during a full, unbroken minute of bellowing in my ear I learned what a wonderful flow of expletives a Flying Corps instructor could possess. Then we turned for home and landing. I at once received a flood of vituperation such as I had never known before.

I tried to explain that I'd not been given a single lesson, but he wouldn't listen, and threatened to have me sent back to my regiment. Then he stalked off. When he was clear, my fellow pupils rolled off their petrol tins with laughter, but I was not that much amused. Some of them had come to the R.F.C. chiefly to get the flying pay, and though this was important to me too, I happened to be desperately keen on flying, and would have hated to lose my long-coveted chance to become a pilot.

This episode, I was soon to learn, was representative of the casual and erratic standards of instruction then prevailing in the R.F.C. Fortunately Lascelles put in a good word. I continued under him, met with no difficulties, and made rapid progress. Later I was to look back and realise that he was the best of my several instructors. I was fortunate, too, to be taught on a machine modified for dual instruction, for in the unmodified type, the pupil sat in the rear seat, and leant over the shoulders of the instructor in front to grasp the spectacles, but never touched the rudder. Very primitive, but it had to work, and somehow it did.

Twelve days after my ticking off, at six in the morning, after six circuits and landings, Lascelles climbed down and told me to do a circuit solo, and to land near him, as he didn't intend to walk back all the way to the sheds. With five hours' dual behind me I had no qualms. I was so busy concentrating on landing close to the solitary figure waiting for me in the middle of the vast aerodrome that I forgot to be elated. I came down twenty yards from him, trundled to a halt, he got in, taxied to the tarmac, and sent me off again to do a half-hour trip.

On this second flight I was able to climb up and away and take stock. I had done my first solo—my first two solos! I was in charge of an aeroplane, piloting it around Salisbury Plain at fifty-five miles

Above: Avro 'Huns' of 66 Squadron at Filton, 1916. Author in centre
Below: Author and B.E.2c, 66 Squadron

Above: Taxi-ing incident. R.E.7 and Avro, Filton
Centre: R.E.7 landing crash, Filton
Below: The Pup lands too fast. La Gorgue, 46 Squadron

an hour, at the satisfying height of 2,000 feet. All I had craved for during the past six or seven years had come to pass. At last I could fly!

My mind flashed back to those days long before the war, when names like Blériot, Cody, Roe, Pegoud, Sopwith, Grahame-White and the brothers Wright filled my gallery of heroes. The days of the Flying Cathedral, the Antoinette, the Blériot monoplane, the Voisin biplane. The days when I would readily cycle half a hundred miles to see the strange wonderful sight of men swooping through the air like great birds. The days when everything to do with flying had for me, as for hundreds of other dreaming youngsters, the quality of magic.

I longed to learn to fly, but my father had recently died and there was no money to pay the fees. When the war came in August 1914 I volunteered for training as a pilot in the R.F.C., but was told that only those who had gained their Royal Aero Club brevet could be considered. I tried to enlist in the Corps as a mechanic, with the notion of one day being promoted to pilot, but learned that only qualified tradesmen were wanted. So I joined a university O.T.C., and in February 1915 was commissioned in the 13th Sherwood Foresters. Within a month I applied for a transfer to the R.F.C., but was snootily rebuffed by the battalion adjutant.

But Fate was with me. In the autumn I was placed on a draft for the Dardanelles, but a few days before we were due to sail I met with a motor-cycle accident that left me unconscious for thirty-six hours. The severe concussion ruled me out for overseas for some time, and after sick leave I took what seemed a suitable opportunity to apply again for a transfer, and once more was told not to be a nuisance.

Meanwhile in France the R.F.C. was suffering heavy losses, and the urgent call came for more pilots and observers. On Cannock Chase, where the 13th Sherwoods were then stationed, I learned in May 1916 that commanding officers had been ordered not to obstruct volunteers. Next day, with what I know must have been a very smug expression, I made my third application to the frowning adjutant. A week or two later I was called to pass a medical board. A few weeks later still came my transfer to the 1st Sherwoods on temporary attachment to the R.F.C., an attachment that was to last nearly thirty years.

I said good-bye to footslogging, and reported to St Patrick's Hall at Reading University, to attend the 10th Ground Training Course. Here among other things I 'learned' air photography, meteorology, map reading, which I had been teaching for eighteen months, and Morse, at which I was far quicker than the instructor, having been battalion signals officer.

From Reading I had come to Netheravon. And now the landmark of my first solo was over. During the next few days, I did three more hours' solo without incident, except for a taxi-ing crash. The Farman was tricky to taxi downwind. On the tarmac, the mechanic had given me the all clear to taxi out for take-off, and I was trundling along on an uncertain course downwind when I realised that ahead of me was another Rumpety returning to the sheds. I just couldn't avoid it, and we met head on, the two projecting nacelles barely an inch apart.

In the other nacelle were a pupil and Lascelles, who calmly leant over to my cockpit and switched off my engine. Had the nacelles crushed into each other there would have been an unpleasant mess of broken limbs or worse. I was absolved of blame, as I had been given the all clear, but one of my nine lives had gone!

During my three hours on Rumpetys I acquired the assurance of blissful ignorance to such a degree that on the impulse of the moment I ventured to land in the staked enclosure around Stonehenge, barely five miles from the aerodrome. Nobody appeared and I took off, with nothing more to show than the secret satisfaction of having done something quite irrational. Later, as other pupils began to do the same thing as a routine, the custodian grew wise. As soon as he saw a plane manœuvring to land, he ran out and waited for it, ready to demand payment for a ticket of admission!

Like most of those who flew Rumpetys, I formed a condescending affection for them, for they were safe, slow and amiable. And after I left Netheravon I was able to judge by later comparisons that 24 Squadron was well run, with sensible instructors, and even the Major, who knew his job as C.O., could be forgiven for his outburst at me, for I learned quite a lot from his vocabulary of expletives which was to be useful when I, in turn, became an instructor.

From 24 Squadron I went to No 66 Squadron at Filton to be taught to fly Avros and B.E.s. The change from the immense openness of Netheravon was pronounced, for Filton was practically a suburb of Bristol, and the home of the Bristol Aeroplane Company, whose sheds took up a large slice of the tarmac, and whose pilots were constantly testing planes, including the new two-seater, of which much was later to be heard. The aerodrome was small, with a public road on one side and a deep railway cutting on another.

Even more notable was the change in aeroplanes, for the Avro was a tractor, powered by a Gnôme monosoupape rotary engine. This was controlled not by a throttle, like the Renault of the Farman, but by a switch in the top of the joystick, by which you 'blipped' the engine on and off sufficiently often to keep it running until you were ready to take off. If you paused too long, alarming sheets of flame from the ejected petrol enveloped the engine and cowling until you hastily blipped again.

Instead of the 'spectacles', there was a 'stick' control column, much to be preferred. The pupil sat in the front seat, from which, when practising landings, he could scarcely see the ground. More, as shouting was out of the question in the air, the instructor could give his orders only by waggling the joystick, a form of communication which had its limitations, and which led to many misunderstandings, not least the frequent doubt as to who was piloting.

I found the controls unexpectedly stiff, but somehow made sufficient headway after four and a half hours' dual, never anything but circuits and landings, to be sent solo. I took off unconcernedly enough, but at once ran into trouble, for as I began a turn I had a horrible feeling that the controls had come unstuck. I soon realised that the fault lay in me, in being ham-fisted, for the controls were feather light, both joystick and rudder. But I had never had this feel of sensitivity of control before, and I quickly understood why. Throughout my dual, the instructors had kept a hand on the joystick and both feet on the rudder bar.

On my second solo a few days later I took off full of confidence, but immediately lost it, for the engine suddenly spluttered and stopped. I had no idea what I ought to do. It didn't occur to me to put the nose down and attempt an emergency landing. I'd never been given a practice forced landing, or even told what to do if the engine failed during take-off. No one had ever stalled the Avro in the air to show me what it felt like. Fortunately I did not attempt to turn back to the aerodrome, the one sure way of effecting a lethal crash, though again, no one had ever warned me against it.

There was a line of trees ahead, and I vaguely felt I ought to get over them somehow. I edged the joystick back, but the Avro did not like my trying this when the engine was not running. She stalled, a wing dipped, and she flicked into a spin. I saw the ground rushing up alarmingly, but remember nothing more, for the crash knocked me out.

When I came to in hospital, my face swathed in bandages, and two of my nine lives gone, I learned I was not held to blame, as an inlet valve had broken. Nobody thought to tell me how I should have avoided stalling. After sick leave, I had twenty minutes' dual, during which the Avro resumed its previous stiffness, then I set off to teach myself to fly. I had never been shown a steep turn, much less a vertical one, while a loop was unknown, except when performed by the rasher type of pupil at great altitudes well away from the aerodrome. I joined their company, found it all surprisingly easy, and grew to realise what a fine plane the Avro was, even when underpowered with its 50 h.p. Gnôme.

Of course nobody tried a spin, for this would have been a suicidal act. Nobody knew how to get out of one, and anyway, this was too reliable a way of being killed accidentally, which was one of the unsettling things at Filton, especially compared with accident-free Netheravon. Filton saw fatal crashes every few days, and usually through mysterious spins into the ground when taking off. Flat spins we called them, and they happened on B.E.s, sometimes right in front of our eyes as we lounged around the tarmac. But nobody knew why.

The instructors put these crashes down to sheer clumsy piloting, and so there it was, hanging over us—if you did a flat spin it was just too bad, practically an act of God. There seemed to be a funeral every week, and as the pupils still alive had to follow and act as pall-bearers, it was rather depressing, but it became something of a routine journey to the cemetery at Clifton, especially as the band played always the same funeral march, and so after two or three burials one got used to it. Afterwards I learned that the same sort of thing was happening at most R.F.C. stations, and for the same reason—poor instruction. Not without reason did we feel that for R.F.C. learners, the war, considered in terms of casualties, began in England.

After five hours' solo on Avros I was considered safe enough to be put on to B.E.s. To me, these were the real thing, war planes, in use in France, the ones I would probably have to fly there. (Looking back, I still can't understand how incredibly ignorant we all were about these wretched machines.) After fifty minutes of circuits and landings in a B.E.2d, during which I allowed for the probability that the instructor was clutching the controls most of the time, I went solo.

I noticed, as I had noticed before on other people's first solos, that the blood-wagon, as we called the ambulance, which always stood by ready on the tarmac, started its engine as I taxied out. And I was not too happy, because the day before, a pupil called Pechell had done a fatal flat spin taking off on *his* first solo. We—the pupils waiting on the tarmac—watched him swing round at 100 feet and dive into the roof of the hangar behind us. I was among the first to reach the crash, and helped to lift him out. I asked, 'Is he badly hurt?' and the ambulance N.C.O. said calmly, 'Oh, he's dead, sir.' It was the first time I'd handled a dead body, and it shook me, especially as I'd been on the razzle with him the previous evening in Bristol.

I had Pechell in my mind as I took off, but everything went well, and I made a good landing in the middle of the aerodrome. Three hours later, in the afternoon, I took off again, in another B.E.2d, this time feeling perfectly sure of myself. As soon as I was about 100 feet up, she started to veer to the right. I applied gentle left rudder and bank to ease her straight, as I would have done on the Avro, but the veer became a swing, the right wing dipped, and I knew it had happened to me!

Suddenly the machine took control, swung round on a flat turn, and dived with engine full on towards the ground. I had no time even to switch off. I was sure I was a dead man, and went through the breath-catching dread of being smashed up like Pechell and the others.

But something told me what to do. I stiffened myself back in my seat, legs braced straight against the rudder bar, arms pressed hard on to the fairing in front of me. As we hit, I distinctly remember hearing myself shouting something—God knows what it was. The machine crashed almost vertically into the ground, fifty yards in front of the tarmac. I sat there for some seconds, stunned with shock. Apart from gashes to my gloved hands, which had driven two inches into the edge of the three-ply fairing, I was not physically hurt. The blood-wagon was already there and the orderlies helped me out of the pile of debris.

Though unhurt, I was dazed for some time, and I just didn't know why it had happened. I just felt that three of my nine lives had now been used up. Before I could get back to normal, I was called to the squadron commander's office. There I was savaged for writing off another machine in a careless crash. I fumed with resentment and anger.

'You bloody idiot, do you think I did it on purpose?'

This is not what I said, I'm afraid, though I would have given a month's flying pay to do so. I wanted to protest that Pechell and the rest had done exactly the same, and nobody knew why. But I dared say nothing, for he was threatening me—'One more crash and you go back to your regiment!'

This threat was frequently made, and was forever hanging over our heads like some 'bluddy bugaboo', as a K.O.Y.L.I. pupil put it, which only made us sore, for most crashes were due to ignorance. Certainly not all instructors were bad—some, like Lascelles, were very good—but half of them were, for one reason or another, unfitted for the work.

Even as uninformed 'Huns', as all instructors everywhere called their pupils, we quickly sorted them out. Some were beginners too, and just didn't know. Some were not even confident pilots, unable to do a vertical turn, and shying off aerobatics. Many were reluctant to entrust their lives to ham-fisted pupils, and never surrendered full control. Some were nervy after active serve, and some, it was rumoured, were throw-outs from squadrons in France, where they had failed to make the grade. But mostly the fault was that they simply didn't know how to teach.

There was no instruction technique, no standard method. Nobody could explain in simple, practical terms how a plane was piloted. There was no communication between instructor and pupil in the air. It was obvious to us all that instructors should have been taught their job. There were competent instructors at the civil flying schools at Hendon and Brooklands, who were engaged mostly in teaching novice *pilots* to get the R.A.C. brevet, but these should long ago have been assembled into a school to give crash courses to R.F.C. novice *instructors*.

It was not an instructor but another pupil, more advanced than me, who had learned the hard way, who put me right about the B.E.s. All of them were heavy on the control, and it was useless to try coaxing them as on the Avro. You had to bully them. As soon as you felt that pull to the right taking off, you had to correct firmly, with strong opposite rudder and bank. Trying to correct gently only encouraged the spin.

Resuming my flying after thirty minutes of the usual circuits and landings, I made quick progress, and passed successively to other B.E. types—the 2b, with warping wings which sent every bump with a kick to the joystick, the 2c, the 2e and the B.E.12. This single-seater version, with a 150 h.p. engine, which was supposed to be Britain's answer to the German Albatros D–II, was a laughable failure in France except to those who were killed on it. In the safe skies of England the B.E.12 was pleasant enough to fly, though unmanœuvrable because of the strong inherent stability common to all B.E.s.

During the second half of December I carried out the several tests for my 'wings'—height, air fighting by camera gun, bomb-dropping (minus bombs) by Batchelor mirror, artillery observation (in one half-hour flight!), photography, cross-country, the lot. None of these tests was remarkable except the cross-country on a B.E.12, when I started out at midday on Christmas Eve, on what should have been a two-hour trip, and did not return until January 6th, having had five forced landings, one on the Lambourn Downs, two on Salisbury Plain and two on the outskirts of Devizes, all caused by a faulty magneto. I was lucky to do no damage, but the first pilot to take up the plane after my return met the same trouble, and wrote it off completely when he tried to land it on an oak tree.

The tests all completed, the day came when I knew my wings were certain, and there was just that little job to do under Clifton Bridge. This accomplished, I was now qualified for overseas, but the Medical Board, because of the Avro crash concussion, following on that of the year before, decided on a spell of Home Service. This was my luck, for otherwise I would have arrived in France in excellent time to be one of the poor devils flying B.E.s in the Battle of Arras, who were shot down by the dozen by Richtofen and other well-mounted German fighter pilots.

After a week's course at the Aerial Gunnery School at Hythe where I learned to handle machine-guns, a point that nobody had thought of so far, I was sent to No 40 Training Squadron at Port-meadow, by Oxford, to be trained as a scout pilot. The scout was the Sopwith Pup, but for nearly three months I was not allowed near one. Instead I put in thirty hours on Avros, teaching myself aerobatics, even the spin, for by now the secret had been solved, and we all knew how to get into one and how to get out. We also did air fighting and formation flying and other exercises that had never been heard of at Filton. The instructors here were on the ball, but did not give dual, merely told us what to do.

Meanwhile, because of the demand for pilots in France, other pupils were being made to put in flying time to qualify for posting overseas, and in the silliest way, sometimes eight hours a day, just flying round and round. Normally, at this time, fifteen hours' solo meant that you were considered fit to meet any Hun, with the result that about one in four of those who went into action with this experience were shot down in their first patrols. I was more fortunate, for I had already done over fifty hours' solo.

At last, on April 24th, I did my first solo on a Pup, and at once realised that all the machines I had flown till now were indeed just machines, even the Avro. For the Pup was a dream to fly, so light on the control, so effortless to handle, so sweet and amenable, and so eagerly manœuvrable that you found yourself doing every kind of stunt without a thought — loops, sideslip landings, tail slides, rolls, spins. And she was just as manœuvrable up high, at 15,000 feet and above.

The only thing that troubled me was air sickness, due in part to the continuous stunting and in part to the smell of burnt castor oil, thrown out by the rotary Le Rhône engine — nearly as bad as the floods thrown out by the Avro's Gnômes.

After nineteen hours on Pups my time at Portmeadow ended. A Medical Board passed me fit, I had my last flight on May 12th, and went over to France on May 16th, where after a short spell in the Pilots' Pool at St Omer I was posted to fly Pups with No 46 Squadron.

THREE
TWENTY-FOUR HOURS

Just as I was telling myself that another ten minutes in my warm sleeping-bag wouldn't do me any harm, the door of the squadron office opened and Major Babington entered.

'Time you were up and about, Lee,' he stated. 'Any calls from Wing?'

'No, sir,' I answered, scrambling hastily from the bag. 'No standby calls. Nothing at all.' I was four-fifths clothed, as I'd removed only my boots and puttees and tunic, and of course my Sam Browne, before sliding into the bag four hours earlier. As orderly officer, I wasn't allowed to undress during the night, in fact during the twenty-four hours of duty, as anything might happen calling for instant action, even during the hours of darkness—such as those bombs soon after midnight!

The major went out and left me to it. I was not surprised to see him appear at the early hour of five o'clock, for he'd been around on the tarmac several times when I was on dawn patrol at four. He saw us off most mornings, even after a late binge, and we thought a lot of him for it.

As I fastened the Sam Browne belt and roughly rolled the valise, ready for my batman to collect before seven, I remembered that I was not on a flying job this morning, not even on standby. After I had inspected the men's breakfasts at seven, for the second morning running, I could make for the Mess, have my own breakfast in comfort, and wash and shave in good time to hand over to the next for duty at eight. Then I would be free until two o'clock, when I was due for a D.O.P., and would meanwhile be able to dodge the hot sun with a few spells in the River Lys.

Quite different from yesterday, I reflected, as I stood outside the office watching the major stroll to the tarmac, where the routine patrol from 'A' Flight, with engines running, was all ready to set off. Yesterday at this time I was in the air. With Eberlin, I'd been detailed the evening before for standby from four o'clock. We'd got up before dawn and were waiting in the Mess for our hard-boiled eggs when the telephone rang. It was of course the orderly officer speaking from the squadron office—a call for us already—a Crossley on the way! It arrived as I put the phone down, and we'd rushed over to the hangars immediately, and in a foul temper too, for nothing is more infuriating than to go out to do battle in the skies on an empty stomach.

The O.O. awaited us with the glad news that an enemy artillery-spotting plane was at work east of Neuve Chapelle at an estimated height of 5,000 feet. Cursing the too-energetic Huns, we taxied out and were off the ground by 4.15. Dawn had just broken, and as we climbed south-eastwards the sun's first rays appeared behind the dark masses of cumulus stretching high overhead.

Usually on these two-seater chases we found when we reached the area where the Hun was supposed to be that he wasn't there, either because he'd finished his job and gone home, or because he'd seen us and withdrawn eastwards, where he would wait until we'd gone away. This time the Hun was around, but he'd watched us arrive and retreated in good order south-eastwards, and as I was still in a black mood over my missed egg, we pursued him for several miles, firing bursts at hopelessly long range until he suddenly dived low and drew away.

I wheeled west and returned to the Lines, climbing hard and keeping well clear of the archie battery at La Bassée, which we much respected for its accuracy. We approached the belt of trenches, and around Lens found a fierce artillery strafe in full swing, though there were no German planes to be seen, and only a couple of our R.E.8s, engaged in spotting. I had no idea what it was all about. We never did know what was happening in this war until we read about it in the newspapers, even though we might have taken part in the happening.

I was still disgruntled, not entirely about the egg but because, like every other fighter pilot, I had no great love for the standby system, though I knew the idea was sound, as we didn't wear out our engines and ourselves doing endless standing patrols, such as during the week preceding the Battle of Messines, when thirteen of us did eighty-seven hours' flying in one day, and McDonald alone did fifty in the week, while even I managed nearly forty. Now, with only one flight doing standing patrols, and the other two standby—flights taking turn and turn about—the demands on us and our machines had lessened considerably.

But what we chiefly disliked about standby was the waiting around for a call. We had begun them just before the squadron was transferred from the 11th to the 10th Wing, and at first each pair of pilots was on standby for six hours at a stretch, all of which they spent loafing outside the squadron office. As there was nothing for us—the pair on standby and the pair next for duty—to sit on, we tried to manage with bricks, but an hour of this made us almost unfit to fly. Later we were given a bench, and were put on two-hour spells, with the result that if there were numerous calls we could find ourselves on standby duty several times a day, and this in practice meant that we were on duty, or next for duty, all through the daylight hours.

The standby system had come in May through a new hush-hush organisation, a chain of interception units sited a few miles behind our Lines. One of them was at the edge of our aerodrome, behind the office, a small hut which was an Aeroplane Compass Station, with a couple of eighty-foot masts, very handy for circling planes to run into. In the hut two R.E.s sat with earphones by a mysterious box of tricks listening in to German machines using wireless on artillery shoots. They telephoned the compass bearings to Army Wing Headquarters, which, with cross-bearings from adjacent stations, obtained intersections. These they phoned to the standby squadron, where us 'poor ginks', as our Canadian, Barrager, put it, had to dash off and do the dirty work.

On the occasions when the intersection was not a phantom, but a Hun who had gone east at our approach, we usually carried out a patrol, for it was better to do two hours' flying than return to a hard bench. But this time I decided to teach the wary Hun a lesson. I led the way north, turned east at 10,000, zigzagged through some indifferent archie, then came round in a wide circle, slipping from cloud to cloud, back towards La Bassée. As I expected, the Hun, a greeny-mottled D.F.W., was on his job again, and drawing closer I rocked my wings and started a dive. Because we were coming from the east the observer wasn't watching our way and didn't see us, but the local archie battery did, and sent up a warning salvo alongside him. He immediately dived steeply southwards, and once more we pursued him in vain.

By now we had been up nearly an hour. The sky was clouding over and masking the rising sun, which made it easier for us to pull off a surprise attack provided we could find something to go for. I turned north again, keeping well east of the Lines, out of archie range. Ten minutes later, when at 11,000 over Pérenchies, I saw two L.V.G.s coming side by side from the north, about 700 feet below us. Experience had taught me that while even a single well-handled two-seater could be tricky to attack when approached from astern and above, which gave the observer a steady target, two two-seaters could be positively dangerous even for a pair of scouts, for they gave each other cover against both astern and under-belly approaches.

But I had worked out this problem with Eberlin previously. I pointed to the right-hand machine, and we swung round to the eastwards with the intention of making a flank attack on converging lines, when the observer couldn't shoot at us both at once, and the other observer's fire was masked. But as we wheeled in a wide curve, a Hun archie battery opened up on us, and followed us round the curve with annoying persistence. Then, when Eberlin was 200 yards out on my flank, and we were about to begin our concerted dive, archie stopped.

I knew what that could mean, and hastily looked back over my right shoulder, but found nothing there, then over my left. Due east, over Lille, I saw, high up against a vast bank of grey cloud with the flaring morning sun behind, a swarm of dark silhouettes, and they were already on the way, which was why archie had so suddenly ceased fire.

In that brief glimpse I counted ten, but Eberlin afterwards said he reckoned twelve. Too many for us to loiter around for, and I swung west, with no further thought for the L.V.G.s, which pressed on southwards. I didn't really care what they did, for the ten Hun scouts were descending in an untidy group, and already firing, as I knew from the streams of tracer and the crackle of bullets, though they must have been inexperienced to open fire at such long range. But there was nothing to be done except dive steeply towards the Lines while we had the chance.

Making sure that Eberlin was diving too, a hundred yards away on my flank, I looked behind and saw that the Huns, Albatros D–IIIs as usual, were gaining rapidly, and their accuracy of fire was improving, as I noticed when a group of bullet-holes appeared magically in my right lower wing. Then, as I steepened the dive and looked back again, there came a rapid succession of archie bursts in front of them. And the balls of smoke were white! Our archie had come to the rescue.

The D–IIIs passed through the barrage, but their dive and aim had been disordered, and their fire was now so wild I couldn't even hear the bullets. We crossed the Lines at 1,000 feet, but the Huns didn't follow, and turned north. We swung north too, climbed to 12,000, then slipped above a convenient string of clouds eastwards for about five miles, and steered south, hopping still from cloud to cloud, on the look-out for another two-seater, and also for the ten Albatroses.

Suddenly Eberlin rocked his wings and pointed down. There, right below us, was another D.F.W., brown and yellow, and I had missed it. I gave the attack signal, and dipped into a dive to attack from three-quarters astern, Eberlin at once pulling out to my right flank. I thought, We will make sure of this one, and I held fire, hoping the observer would not spot us. The plane grew larger and larger in the Aldis sight as I went hurtling down with two-thirds throttle.

Strangely in these attacks on two-seaters I was seldom in the state of quivering excitement that always overcame me when about to engage in a dog-fight with a formation of fighters. Then, one had to twist and turn for one's life, as well as for victory, with chance for only brief bursts of fire at fleeting targets, but in a dive on a two-seater, even on a curve, one kept the sight glued to the apparently stationary target in a kind of calm detachment, hoping that the pilot wouldn't jink and disturb one's aim.

I was now close enough to see that the observer was looking downwards. We were at 200 yards range and the pilot's cockpit was at the centre of my Aldis. I pressed the trigger gently, and, as the tracers flashed down, glimpsed those from Eberlin's gun coming in at an angle from the right. The startled observer swung his head up, saw us, grabbed his guns, and in a second was blazing defiantly at us. I continued firing in bursts of twenty or so, then suddenly the pilot dropped into a steep dive, with sudden full engine, as I could see from the spume of black smoke from the upright exhaust pipe. At this moment my Vickers stopped. A jam! Cursing wildly, I banged the cocking handle with the hammer, but it refused to go down.

The Hun was now diving nearly vertically, and although I had pushed my throttle wide open, he quickly pulled away, with Eberlin, still firing, in hopeless pursuit. It was possible that one of us had winged the pilot, but the machine was under control, and merely to drive it down for a time counted for nothing. I followed on, fruitlessly, for we had lost him, and he was already almost out of sight. I was not very pleased with my shooting, or with Eberlin's either, for the Hun was a sitter, and we had let him escape by sheer bad markmanship.

Eberlin joined me, and I turned north-west, climbing up once more over a vast mountain of cumulus, its crest transformed by the mounting sun into peaks of gold. As I hammered vainly at the obstinate gun, I looked to the north-east, where not far away was another sunlit cloud-top, and around it a group of black specks was gambolling. Our friends the ten Albatroses, perhaps, doing what I liked doing. Although we were still nearly five miles over and my gun was out of action, I couldn't resist, and we spent five joyous minutes plunging side by side into the deep valleys, exploring the dark crevasses and storming the vertical cliffs.

Then we continued westwards, and as patrol time was now up, span down together, engines off, to 2,000, and went decorously back to La Gorgue. As soon as I had thrown off my flying gear, and reported to the office, the orderly sergeant appeared to tell me that Williams, the orderly officer whom I was due to relieve at eight, had just gone on a standby call and would I take over now? And there was a job for me in ten minutes' time—the men's breakfasts.

I hastened to put on a collar and tie, and the Sam Browne, which was the O.O.'s badge of office, for we seldom wore one at any other time while in camp. At seven o'clock I duly appeared at the messing tent with the sergeant and went through the usual routine. 'Tenshun!' by the sergeant, 'Any complaints?' by me, dead silence by the men, then 'Carry on!' by the sergeant, and out we went. The sergeant kindly reminded me that it was pay day, and what time would I want transport to fetch the money? I told him, and by then quite ravenous, entered the Mess for my own breakfast, after which I washed and shaved and arranged for Asher, next for duty after me, to hold the fort while I fetched the pay from the field cashier's office at Hinges.

At 8.30, as no Crossley was available, I set out for Hinges, some twenty-five miles to the south-west, in a P. & M. motor-cycle and side-car. I told the driver not to dawdle, and he gladly took me at my word, pelting along the winding road like a madman, swerving in and out of traffic with hair-raising tyre screeches and taking every bend at such speed that I spent most of the trip leaning half out of the sidecar to keep it down. But I daren't say a word. I couldn't even clutch at the top edges of the sidecar. How could I ask him to go slower and so reveal that he was putting the wind up a scout pilot? On the contrary, I had to pretend that I enjoyed it all as much as he did.

However, I survived the double journey, and then, while the corporal clerk was sorting out the money and checking the pay rolls, I inspected the camp with the orderly sergeant who had come on duty at eight. It was quite a route march to go round the whole aerodrome, the men's tents, the cookhouse, the canteen, the messing tent, the latrines, the Sergeants' Mess, the Officers' Mess, and then on the other side of the aerodrome, the hangars, the armoury, the transport lines, the petrol store, and everywhere the fire appliances, two or three of them tested and replaced, and finally the guard, including those at their posts. I found that none of them knew what he had to do in an emergency, such as meeting a spy with a bomb, and as I didn't know either, nor the orderly sergeant, I mentioned it in my report just to keep the Recording Officer on his toes.

At eleven o' clock I took pay parade in 'A' Flight hangar, the one nearest to the office, to the constant noisy accompaniment of engines being run up, and planes taxi-ing and taking off and landing, and in addition the rattle of gun-limbers and other traffic on the cobbled road immediately behind us. As the parade was ending, a message came that the Recording Officer wanted to see me.

'Just in time, Lee,' he said as I entered the office. 'I want you to take my chair for an hour or so while I run into Merville for a haircut.' And off he went, while I sat in his place, with the major working at the other table. He was not what one would call a chatty person, and as I hadn't the nerve to start a conversation, we sat in silence. He at least had work to occupy him, but I just gazed at the wall. Then the phone rang. It was Wing Headquarters, wanting to know something about engine spares, and as I hadn't the slightest notion about anything, I passed the phone to the major. This happened twice more, after which he'd had enough, and went out for a walk. Fortunately not another call came in.

The R.O. returned in good time for me to be collected by the orderly sergeant and taken to the messing tent to do the vital routine again—'Tenshun!'—'Any complaints?'—Silence—'Carry on!' Actually I would have preferred to have sat down and shared the men's luscious, bubbling Lancashire hot-pot instead of returning to the half-hearted curry in my own mess. I would also have loved a swim after lunch, but this was out, some emergency might have arisen while I had my clothes off.

Instead I had to go back to the hangars and do an air-firing practice to check my Vickers after this morning's stoppage, which was a bad one, a faulty tracer having stuck at the back of the barrel and been split by the next round coming in the breech. The target was in a farmer's field across the river, a large ringed board set at forty-five degrees, at which you fired short bursts in long dives. But first you flew low over the nearby fields and waved off the farm workers, mostly women. They were used to the routine and ambled a hundred yards away in the touching belief that they were safe at that distance.

You didn't dive too low or too steeply, and you eased out of the dive smoothly, and not with a sharp jerk as did some Pup pilot at another aerodrome, thereby pulling his wings off. With no enemy fighters to worry about, I did some accurate shooting, and the gun worked as smoothly as if such headaches as stoppages never existed.

As I landed and taxied to 'C' Flight hangar, Pratt, my flight commander, came up and said, 'Hurry and get loaded up again, Lee, you're on an escort job in ten minutes' time.' While the armourers worked feverishly putting in fresh belts of ammunition, I learned that an emergency photographic recco had appeared, and Courtneidge and I had to escort a B.E.2e from 10 Squadron to a target quite a way over the Lines.

We took off at 2.30, as soon as the Quirk, which came from Choc-ques, down by Béthune, appeared over the aerodrome, and followed it to the Lines, flying a few hundred feet above its height of 5,000, which to me offered unpleasant prospects, for there were plenty of low cloud-banks around for archie to register on. As I expected, we were plastered quite savagely when we crossed into Hunland, the black bursts surrounding us continuously as salvo followed salvo, for we could not employ our usual trick of slight evasive action because we were too low, and because we had to stay near the Quirk.

To my amazement, the pilot didn't bother to change course at all, but flew unconcernedly through the bursts of flame and smoke as

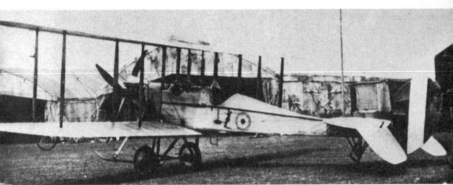

Above: L.V.G. (B55/14).
Unarmed
Centre: B.E.2b with
warped wing control.
Unarmed. 66 Squadron
Right: Aviatik (C
4204/15)

Above: F.E. 2b of 11 Squadron, Arras Front (*Flight International*)
Below: L.V.G. C–II

though they were fireworks. These B.E. pilots obviously became hardened to their risks, but to me, accustomed to not very accurate archie at our normal high altitudes, this particular man's indifference to whether he was hit or not seemed quite suicidal, and I was both surprised and relieved not to be damaged.

Equally hazardous, to me, was the low altitude at which he flew, to which we had to adhere, though we would have stood not the slightest chance against Albatros D–IIIs or any other Hun fighter. As we pressed on to the target, the railway junction at Orchies, well over fifteen miles into German-held territory and so far as I was concerned, practically on the outskirts of Berlin, not a minute passed without me twisting my neck to search for Huns, but miraculously none appeared, not even when the pilot of the B.E. took his photographs, making leisurely runs over the target at 5,000 while we circled just overhead.

I resumed this ceaseless searching, and I knew that Courtneidge was doing the same, when we set out on the return journey, and at last, inevitably, spotted four Huns catching us up from the east, behind. Courtneidge saw them too, and rocked his wings warningly. I have seldom felt so vulnerable, not only because I was flying an obsolescent Pup in company with an obsolete Quirk, but because we were tied to it, and could not start our usual manœuvrings to receive the attack, for this would have meant leaving our charge to fly on alone.

The Huns, which I could now see were V-strutters, began their dive, and I found myself tingling with the usual preliminary funk, for such I suppose it was, though normally it vanished the moment I pressed the trigger. And now I had something to be windy about, as we waited in suspense for the tracer, unable to do anything but zigzag over the B.E., knowing that it was not our own lives we had to think of but those of its crew, with their precious load of photographs.

Even the B.E. pilot started jinking as the tracer began stabbing down towards us, with the crack-ak-ak of bullets passing so close that I had to bank steeply into a circle to avoid presenting a static target. The B.E.'s observer was firing long bursts, switching from one Hun to another. Then they were upon us, and I made ready for a duel, knowing we were done for, but knowing also that we had to put up a fight.

Then to my astonishment, instead of levelling out and starting a scrap, the four of them dived on past us and disappeared below. I couldn't believe my eyes, and searched above to see if another formation was on its way. But the sky was clear. Those four D–IIIs could have made mincemeat of two Pups at 5,000 feet, and the B.E. would then have been a gift, but I didn't get too agitated about it, we were all alive.

We continued the journey in something of a daze. Archie was waiting for us, no doubt eagerly, for there was a strongish westerly wind to slow us down. Our outward passage was almost a pleasure jaunt compared with what we now experienced as we approached the Lines, well north of the La Bassée battery. Suddenly woof! woof! crump! crump! then what seemed half the archie in France came up at us, high explosive, shrapnel, flaming onions, the lot. The onions were quite frightening, chains of green spheres of burning phosphorous, turning over and over as they slowly rose, apparently determined to wrap themselves round your fuselage, and when they didn't, and passed above, you felt you had to flee in case they fell on you.

But the B.E. pilot flew as straight a course as if he'd been on a cross-country in England. I concluded that the crews of B.E.s and R.E.s and other photographic and reconnaissance and bombing planes were so accustomed to being ruthlessly archied at low altitudes that they became fatalistic, like the infantryman—what's the use of dodging?—if it's got your number on it, you've had it!

Three times shells burst so close to me that the Pup lurched over sideways, and I was engulfed in pungent, eye-stinging smoke. I saw gashes appear in my wings where chunks of shrapnel had torn through, and when I got home and examined the machine I realised that I'd never been so severely archied before. And yet, apart from a couple of cut bracing wires and some ribs in a port wing, and a splintered spar which meant a new starboard lower wing, there was no vital damage. And I wasn't even touched. Our trip cost the Germans quite a lot of money in explosives, but as we were soon to learn they did get results.

We crossed the trenches at 4,000, and waved to the B.E. pilot and observer, who waved back as they left us and swung south-west for Chocques. We could not know that within minutes the two of them would be dead. The next day we learned that both the pilot and his observer, a sergeant, had been doing their last trip before posting to home establishment. Their baggage was packed except for the needs of one more night with 10 Squadron. We did not know that the pilot had been hit by archie, and when he waved good-bye he was beginning to lose consciousness, with the result that a minute or so later he ran into the cable of one of our balloons. The machine dived into the ground, and both of them died of their injuries soon after being removed from the wreckage.

Unaware of this tragedy, we landed in good spirits over our unexpected escape from the four Albatroses, whom we could only assume were a bunch of pupils from a training school trying out their hand for the first time, and were met with the information that the squadron was being favoured with a visit by a general in an hour's time. Now I understood why the R.O. had suddenly decided to get his hair cut.

The general arrived at four o'clock, and we stood by our Pups lined up on the tarmac while he passed along and spoke to us. He had wings with a couple of ribbons below, and his manner was friendly even to low forms of life like us pilots. When he came to me I saluted smartly and opened my mouth to say 'Good morning, sir' but came to a halt after 'Good' as I couldn't decide whether it *was* morning or maybe afternoon. By the time I'd worked out that as my last meal had been curry, and must thus have been lunch, and therefore I should say 'Good afternoon', he'd gone on, doubtless thinking me a half-wit. These very early patrols and double breakfasts, the spasms of hard work alternating with spells of idleness, and especially the boredom of hanging around for hours on standby, made one lose all sense of time.

I'd no idea who the general was, for nobody bothered to tell us, and I wasn't sufficiently interested to ask. Nor was anybody else. Until a few days ago I'd never realised who our last Wing Commander was, and I only learned this because he was mentioned in Daily Routine Orders over the squadron's switch from 11th to 10th Wing. He was Lieutenant-Colonel G. B. Stopford, and the new one was Lieutenant-Colonel Wilfrid Freeman, and so far as I know I'd never seen either of them. I found this odd, compared with my old infantry battalion, where everybody down to the fatiguemen knew the colonel, and even the brigadier, at least by sight. I suppose our sad ignorance existed because we were interested only in our flying and in the squadron, and not in the remote people higher up, especially the staff. Maybe that operated in reverse, too!

As soon as the general had gone, I had to get down to the task of censoring the airmen's letters, which I should have done in the morning, if I'd had the time. Fortunately I was aided by the four standby victims waiting outside the office. I never much liked doing this job, for I felt I was prying into other people's private lives, which of course I was. The intimate letters to wives and sweethearts, the ones with real heartaches, touching on love, jealousy, children, illness, money worries and so on, one skimmed through hurriedly, for it was too much like peeping through a keyhole.

But fortunately most writers disposed of their private affairs in a perfunctory way, in set formal phrases, though one never knew whether they avoided expressing intimacies and emotion because they knew we would have to read them, or because they just couldn't find the words, or simply because they were incapable of feeling deep emotion about anything.

Most writers became interesting, to us, when they dealt with the squadron, and this was where the need for censorship might have come in, though it never did in my experience, for what they wrote was innocuous enough. They were as proud to be in a Scout squadron as we were, and every fitter and rigger boasted of what *my* pilot had done, gave largely imaginary accounts of our patrols and fights, and was highly braced, despite the additional work involved, when his particular machine came back full of holes.

As the five of us finished the last bunch of letters, the orderly ser-geant came up and saluted. I got up without a word, and we walked side by side to the waiting Crossley, which took us to the men's mess-ing tent for the evening-meal inspection. Once more the familiar, futile but essential routine—'Tenshun!'—'Any complaints?'—'Carry on!'—then bidding the N.C.O. adieu until Lights Out, I went into the Mess for a drink, for it was now seven o'clock, and I reckoned I deserved one after a good day's work.

But Pratt happened along before I could even give my order, and said, 'Oh, Lee, there's nobody else around, I'm afraid, and I want you to help out by taking up a couple of the new chaps and showing them the Lines. They're on patrol early tomorrow.' The new chaps, Armitage and Thompson, had arrived the day before, and had so far done just round-the-aerodrome flights. The three of us drove back to the hangars, and set off ten minutes later, with me flying Hughes' Pup because mine was still in dock.

The sky was now overcast, with cloud base at 2,000 feet, but with gaps here and there showing wispy, grey masses above. I decided to fly at 2,000, and led the way south to beyond Arras, keeping well on this side of the balloon lines. By the time we turned to come back, the clouds were thinning and there were glimpses of blue sky. I hadn't yet seen another plane, but suddenly from the west, three scouts flying in formation passed across a sizable gap, some 500 feet higher than us.

I gave them a casual glance, thinking they were V-strutter Nieu-ports, then nearly fell out of the cockpit. Black crosses! They were Albatroses, and behind me were two complete innocents! It was at this interesting moment that I remembered I'd neglected to warn them to load their guns before taking off!

Waiting for the three Huns to dive and slaughter us put me on the rack for some seconds, but before I could slink with my charges to the westwards, I realised that the Huns amazingly hadn't spotted us, and were sliding east, in and out of the drifting clouds. Fortunately the new boys hadn't seen them, and so knew nothing, and when we returned home I didn't enlighten them, or, for that matter, anybody else, for I didn't feel too pleased with myself. It took me some time to recover from the shock of seeing Hun fighters on *our* side of the Lines, and especially coming from the west so late and at that low height. To me this was always to remain one of the oddest episodes of my time in France.

When we reached the Mess we found that a binge had started, for 'A' Flight had downed a couple of Huns, their tails were well up, and we all had to join in and make merry, though as orderly dog I had to watch my step, for everybody else might get tipsy, but not me! After dinner there was a sing-song, from which I departed briefly for Lights Out, another futile formality, for they went on again as soon as I'd gone away, and again at eleven, when I went the round of the sentries. This ended at the hangars, and I decided I might as well leave the binge to wear itself out and go to my bed, which my batman had set out for me in the squadron office hours before.

It was after midnight when I slipped into my sleeping bag, and just as I was settling down to sleep I heard the unmistakable deep throb of Mercedes engines. There was nothing new to this, for we had enemy bombers over most evenings, as well as our own going the other way, but suddenly came the roar of exploding bombs, and not far away. I leapt out of bed and rushed outside. Flames were visible to the east, in Estaires, searchlights stabbed the sky, archie shells were bursting vainly overhead. As I watched, four bombs fell beyond the other side of the aerodrome. *That* will put a stop to the binge, was my first thought. One bomb dropped in the River Lys, off to my left, sending up an enormous fountain, like a tall, thin ghost under the starlit sky.

And then I realised that the Huns were throbbing almost directly overhead. Before I could even think of what I should do there came a burst of red flame on the aerodrome straight ahead of me, half a mile distant, and then the crash of the explosion. A second or two later another burst, much nearer. I stood there, becoming more and more petrified at each explosion, as another fell, closer still, and yet another, barely a hundred yards away. They had all dropped on the aerodrome, parallel with the hangars, but well away from them.

The strain of waiting for the fourth bomb to land on me was

rather more than I could bear, and it was an enormous relief to have the orderly sergeant appear a couple of minutes later. He was perfectly calm and collected. When people suddenly started rushing around in the darkness with torches he promptly yelled, 'Put those bloody lights out!' He told me that not one bomb had fallen even on the tarmac, all were on the farmland which was the aerodrome. And there were no casualties, except that the sentry at the post by the end hangar, who'd been taken short and gone out on to the aerodrome, had been caught with his trousers down by the first bomb falling fifty yards away, and was now in the guardroom, behaving in an hysterical manner.

The telephone bell rang. It was the major, to whom I gave the news that the hangars and everything else were unscathed. He said no damage had been done at his end, as the bombs had dropped in open fields. Meanwhile, the sergeant had gone round on another check, and soon he came to report that all was normal, including the agitated sentry. I slipped once more into my bag, and was asleep in seconds. To me it seemed but a few seconds more when I was awakened at a quarter to five by the engines of the early routine patrol being run up by the mechanics on the tarmac, but this was no concern of mine, and I stayed in my bed in a half-doze until that awkward moment when the major entered.

So ended my spell as orderly dog, or, at least, nearly ended, for I still had to inspect the breakfasts. By the time I was clear at eight o'-clock I should have had quite a busy twenty-four hours!

FOUR

HIGH FLYERS

Our orders are Close Offensive Patrol at 18,000 feet. By now I know what kind of arctic temperatures to expect at these heights, even in June, and like my two companions I take elaborate precautions.

We assemble in the 'C' Flight office, and while the patrol leader, Captain Pratt, speaks about his intentions and tactics, I pull on my sheepskin thigh-boots (wool inside), having first put on a second pair of socks (thick ones), then a couple of sweaters under my tunic. I arrange my long muffler carefully round my neck and don my knee-length, wool-lined, fur-collared, leather flying coat, beautifully stained and smelly with castor oil from many hours' exposure to rotary engines.

Next is the unpleasant job of applying a generous layer of whale grease to my face, especially the parts that will be exposed—the cheeks, lips and tip of the nose—for if they are not protected I can be sure of frost-bite. The revolting aroma of the grease will haunt me all through patrol, but that is all part of the high flyer's burden.

Having wiped my hands on cotton waste, I fit my oily, fur-lined leather helmet, reeking even more than the coat of castor oil, and my goggles in their fur-lined mask, first making sure that the lenses are perfectly clean, for in the air specks of dirt will appear to be distant Huns. Then I draw on my leather, wool-lined gauntlets, with a fold-over mitten to keep my fingers less frigid when they're not manipulating controls or the gun. Most of us, including me, wear fine silk undergloves as well.

It is a hot afternoon, and in my polar equipment I am perspiring freely by the time I climb into the open cockpit, a tight fit in the narrow Pup, and tighter still for Odell, who is bulkier than me. Then I fasten the safety-belt, do the routine cockpit drill, start the engine, load the Vickers, and am ready for business.

I taxi out with the others, and soon we are climbing in loose formation north-eastwards. We have a long pull before us, nearly four miles of altitude, and Pratt settles into a steepish angle of ascent which demands full throttle from me to keep in position. As we mount higher into the rarer air, I edge back the fine adjustment which controls the proportions of petrol and air going into the engine, until I produce maximum power, as shown on the rev-counter.

The sky is a chaos of formless clouds up to 5,000 feet, but then come giant banks of cumulus, and as we climb close alongside their flanks our precarious craft seem ridiculously puny against the towering masses piled high on each other, their overhanging tops apparently about to tumble and envelop us. Down below, the familiar pock-marked belt of trenches unfolds. British planes, singly and in formation, move purposefully on their affairs, little black specks against the backdrop of grey and purpling cloud, but we have no interest in what they are doing, our place is much higher in the heavens.

After fifteen minutes' climbing we reach 10,000 feet, and look into the deep, mysterious canyons of the higher crags of the cloud-mountains now shining white and sparkling under an unhindered sun. Another quarter of an hour, and we pass their majestic crests, which rise here and there to 15,000 feet and more. As we slowly mount still higher, we look down on what have now become range after range of icebergs. But soon their snowy peaks are dulled, for a thin sheet of cirro-cumulus is moving swiftly across the sky 2,000 feet above, and its mackerel pattern gradually robs us of most of the sun.

We rise steadily towards this cirrus layer and pass through it to find that we have lifted clear of the highest cloud, and are skimming along in brilliant sunshine. As the cirrus passes further eastwards below us, it becomes a level ocean of rippling white, masking the earth. Above us is the cobalt vault of the limitless sky. The three of us at 20,000 feet are alone in a vast sunlit emptiness.

Three times on the way up from 15,000 feet Pratt has turned temporarily eastwards and fired a few rounds to keep the Vickers from freezing up, a precaution which Odell and I duly followed. Now as he sets his patrol course firmly to the east, he fires half a dozen shots.

I pull clear of him, and press the trigger. A single shot! The cocking handle is down, it is not a jam—my gun has frozen up. I reload and press the trigger, and again comes a single shot. I have to send off four more single rounds before the breech mechanism warms up sufficiently for normal firing. And this although we are supposed to have non-freeze oil! From now on, without waiting for Pratt, I fire five rounds or so every four or five minutes, for to drop into a fight with a frozen gun would not be healthy.

The effort of re-loading several times at this height has tired me, and I sit quietly for a few minutes, or as quietly as I can under the difficulty of getting enough of the rarified air into my lungs. But even this comes second to the purgatory of the cold, for the gun is not the only victim. From 17,000 feet upwards I have been in acute discomfort, as I know my companions are too.

The thick leather flying coat keeps out the wind but not the cold. Nothing keeps out the cold, not my sweaters, nor my extra socks, nor my silk gloves, nor my muffler. The cockpit is so tight that I can't move at all to help keep the blood circulating. But it is my hands that suffer most, for they go quite dead, and all I can do to keep them from becoming just frozen meat is to clap them together fiercely or beat them on my knees.

But now I am furious because I find I have not adjusted the muffler sufficiently snugly round my neck, for there is a slight gap between it and the back of my helmet. In this open cockpit I am exposed not just to the four winds of heaven but to hundreds of them, arctic blasts swirling round the cockpit and round me, and now mostly penetrating halfway down my back. And there is nothing I can do, for though I move the muffler up to plug the gap, each time I turn my head to look out for Huns behind I open it again. The resulting icy gusts are unendurable, but I have to endure them.

In the middle of all this I suddenly manage a smile at the thought of a newspaper article that had thrown us into roars of laughter in the Mess last evening. Some alleged expert portentously disclosed that scout pilots such as us, when flying on very high patrols, wore charcoal-heated asbestos jackets. Somebody in Fleet Street must have met a convincing leg-puller.

My spasm of amusement lasts only a moment. Pratt is still on the climb, to see what height he can reach, I suppose, and is now two or three hundred feet above Odell and me. We are hanging on our props, in climbing position, but just going forward and gaining no more height. My lateral controls are flabby. Odell and I have reached our ceiling, 20,500 on the clock, but Pratt, who as flight commander naturally has the best engine in the flight, manages to get to 21,000. This little experiment over, he descends to 20,000, and we press steadily eastwards at this height, the only human beings in our uncharted universe above the clouds.

As we move along over enemy-held territory, I reflect on the amazing fact that I am here at all, sitting in this flimsy little aeroplane, its supporting wings outstretched, the fabric trembling under the wind, the frail wooden structure held together by the straining, quivering wires, the faithful engine keeping me aloft, yet its beat not even noticed because it is the normal. And as I pilot this obedient machine through the crystal air, I am filled with a sense of mastery over space, over nature, over life itself.

I explore the vast emptiness in which I am a proud but insignificant speck, look up into the violet of the furthest heavens, into the infinite zenith, and blink at the glaring sun, then gaze around me to the faraway horizons, apparently on my level. There comes an awesome feeling of loneliness. I and my companions are utterly remote from our mundane existence on the earth which we cannot even see. The three of us are as one, seemingly stationary, with no sensation of speed, just placed here for always in the void. Everything is still. The engine is soundless. The leader's fluttering pennants are petrified movement. Even time is at a standstill. There is nothing between us and eternity, in space, in time.

Almost in wonder, I realise that I am one of the few thousand human beings in the history of mankind who have been chosen to experience this celestial vision. Compared with ordinary earthbound mortals, I am an Olympian god, enthroned high in the heavens, free, serene, uninvolved. Compared with the wretched millions locked in earthly combat, I and my companions are a winged aristocracy among warriors, looking down on the invisible trenches below in pity and amazement.

But these elevated reflections do not persist for long. The piercing cold regains its first place in my preoccupations, especially when we swing from our southerly beat towards the west, which means more frequent watching behind for the Hun on my tail, which means that damned draught down my back every minute or two. Almost I feel that I would welcome an attack by a bunch of Albatroses to provide some excitement that would raise the temperature a little, and certainly break the monotony. To be flying so high, the only occupants of the skies, with nothing but a shining white ocean of cloud to engage one's interest, and nothing to do but the periodic bouts of gun-warming, can become wearisome.

In a moment of resentment at having to endure such inflictions, I ask myself, Why the devil do we have to do these idiotically high patrols? But of course I know the answer. It is to prevent the high-flying Hun fighters attacking our lower-level fighters, such as Spads and Nieuports, which are there to protect artillery observation and other hardworking planes at lower levels still. And Pups get the top patrols because at these heights their light wing-loading confers the advantage over every other fighter, including the Albatros. And so, despite the cold and rare air, I admit I prefer to meet Huns at 17,000 feet upwards, for then we no longer fight at a disadvantage.

As we fly to the westwards, I realise the vast blanket of cirrus has an edge to the north and west, and I can see the coast beyond, a clear line stretching from the islands of the Scheldt in the north to the mouth of the Seine to the south-west. More, I can see the sea, the English Channel, a silver strip with the fainter line of the English coast beyond. It seems so remote, not so much in distance as in tangibility, that I could be looking at the moon.

We turn east again, and I lose that distant link with the solid earth. But soon comes another, less welcome distraction, for the physical tribulations of flying really high in an open cockpit are not confined merely to being half-frozen. By now, the cold's piercing penetration to my interior has made me realise that I should not have had those two long lime-juices at lunch, even though the heat and the reaction of a long swim in the River Lys gave me so acute a thirst I couldn't resist. But now I regret it.

I hold out for a time, but the call becomes urgent, and I give my reluctant attention to a difficult expedient, with the hope that no Hun will come along at an inconvenient moment. My hands are completely numb, but I pull off my right gauntlet and fumble interminably at opening buttons, which takes quite a time, because my fingers have no sense of touch. Then comes the task of finding the way through a barrier of obstinate underclothes. This achieved, there is the problem of where? The refined procedure is to have a funnel with a rubber tube running to a container on the floor of the cockpit, but most of us just aim at the joystick and hope for the best, the hope being strongest over Hun territory.

Then comes the job of getting things back as they were. When it is all over and the gauntlet is replaced, the effort has exhausted me, and I flop back in my seat panting for several minutes. Of course, the even more difficult predicament is capable of neither solution nor description, but it is a real problem, for the castor-oil fumes that one inhales for hours at a time from the Le Rhône rotary engine constitute a positive purgative. Some of us are obliged not only to avoid fruit and other healthy delicacies but to drink stiff doses of chlorodyne before going on any long, high-flying patrols.

We have now been at 20,000 feet for nearly half an hour, and I suddenly realise that I've had enough of the effort of breathing in the rarified atmosphere. I am heaving all the time, mouth wide open, pumping in the bitingly cold air in quick, lung-flooding gasps. I even forget the cold. My heart is thumping, and I feel almost faint. Just when I know I can stand it no longer, Pratt begins to drop very gradually. Obviously, he is suffering too.

As we ride gently down I see, below and ahead of us, rising out of the white sheet of cirrus, five black specks. Huns at last! Pratt spots them too—he can hardly not do so, for in this virgin sky they are as prominent as the sun. And so are we. They find us at once, swing round and climb towards us. We are 3,000 feet above them, but as they draw nearer they gradually lessen the height gap. Soon I see that they are Albatros V-strutters.

We fire our guns to make sure they are warm. Mine isn't. Once more I have to load and re-load. Once more this slight exertion sets my heart thumping, and I can't say I feel ready for a fight. But Pratt is in no hurry to attack. He has worked out our tactics for just such a situation as this, to exploit the virtues of the lightly loaded Pup against the heavier Albatros, and he lets them go on climbing—the higher they are, the better for us. At 20,000 the Pup can still fly, but the Albatros, when it gets there, can only wallow.

So although even at their present height we should still have the advantage in a dog-fight, they are five to three, and we are at a better advantage if we use our height and lightness to shoot without being shot at. Thus Pratt does not intend to become embroiled in a dog-fight, which is what they are seeking.

Now 1,000 feet below us, they are close enough to be identified as D–IIIs, all gaily painted as usual. But at 19,000 they have reached their useful ceiling. Two of them are a hundred feet higher than the rest, but all are hanging on their props, getting no higher, and looking absurdly like poodles sitting up for tit-bits. Pratt rocks his wings, the signal for attack, for there is no point in waiting longer.

They are watching us, and as we drop into a dive, they scatter. We slide down steeply towards them, and I fire a preliminary burst to make sure the gun is in action. This is our chance if only we can shoot straight. I put the Aldis on to one of them, but can't hold him, because of his erratic swerves. I lift my goggles to get a wider-angle view, but even behind the windscreen the icy blast makes my eyes water, and I drop the goggles again.

When I am 300 feet above them, diving fast, I get my sight momentarily on to one painted blue with green wings, and press the trigger. The tracers flash away, I follow his swerve, still firing until, out of the corner of my eye, I see Pratt zoom up. I immediately follow. The impetus of the dive takes us up again to nearly 200 feet above them. Bad shooting, there are still five.

We dive again. This time I get above and behind a machine painted dappled brown, and I am pumping lead into him at 100 yards range when my gun stops. I zoom up, pulling out the hammer from its socket, as I rise and hit the cocking handle. A number one stoppage. The handle goes down, and I swing over to dive again, but the exertion of hitting the gun has set me gasping, I can't get enough air. As I drop down I see the brown plane going off eastwards, in a shallow descent. I must have hit him, but he's under control, wounded maybe. I have no chance to watch him vanish.

The other Pups are zooming up as I dive. I see a Hun spinning down below the others—Pratt's, I learn afterwards. I fire twenty rounds at the blue and green again, following him in a turn, and just as I zoom up I see the spinner disappear through the cirrus. We are still nearly 200 feet above the remaining three. None of them has yet been able to fire a shot at us, except by hanging briefly on their props. Our curious little battle is being fought out above the background of white cirrus, with only the sun to watch, for nobody on earth can see us.

Suddenly they realise they can't win. We can keep diving on them until our ammunition runs out, and they can't retaliate. Two of them are already out, and the three below know that eventually we'll get them too if they stay where they are. So wisely they turn away in a dive eastwards.

I'm glad to see them go. We are masters of all we survey, but the exertions and excitements at this height, the constant, urgent gasping for air, the frightful cold biting right into my belly, have made me show signs of distress. I feel exhausted, without even the energy to be elated at our little victory. But Pratt is made of tougher stuff. His blood is up, and now that they are on the run and the odds are even, he rocks his wings again and drops into a dive after them, engine full on. Odell and I follow. There's no hope of catching them up unless they level out and wait for us, which as we get down to 17,000 they ought to do, but they don't, they dive even more steeply and disappear through the cirrus. We brush through behind them.

After the brilliant sunlight above, the world below seems dull and heavy, with masses of grey bulging cloud hiding most of the earth. But there are the D–IIIs, 1,500 feet under us, diving, but not steeply now, in a curve towards an island of purpling cumulus. Pratt cuts across their curve, gains distance, dives more steeply, still with engine full on. The Huns turn a little towards us, and our dive becomes almost vertical. The Pup throbs, I feel the wings shuddering, and I don't like it. I've had this experience before, and have decided that the good old Pup takes exception to being dived vertically under full power. However, the wings don't come off. We are still gaining, and they don't seem to know we're after them.

We are down to 11,000 feet. Pratt opens fire at 300 yards and I and Odell follow. The Huns hear the shots, and swerve round, then lead us into a mad chase round the side of another mountain of cloud. I'm glad they're not asking for a fight—at this height their better performance and armament would tell. I much prefer to continue taking long-range pot-shots, except that unfortunately we don't seem to be hitting them.

Suddenly they turn towards the nearest mass of cloud and are engulfed in it. One moment they are there, a target we're shooting at, and the next they aren't, like a conjuring trick. But why? Surely we can't have hit them all? False hope! A formation of five Spads has dived on them from the west, and they have neatly escaped. The Spads pull up at the cloud and swarm angrily at its face, but there is no point in pursuit into so monstrous a mass of blinding mist.

We level out, and Pratt leads us quietly southwards. Like Odell and me, he is feeling the punishing effects of our sudden descent. We are now at 9,000, and have dropped over 10,000 feet in about a minute, when normally, from 20,000, we come down gradually by stages, with a few minutes' level flight at each stage, to adjust ourselves to the higher air pressure and temperature. But now our almost vertical two-mile dive has left me dazed with the splitting pain in my head and throbbing eardrums. My eyes are slits, seeing only shooting stars. My heart is still racing. Nausea floods over me, and I prepare to vomit over the side of the cockpit.

But I don't, for my attention is distracted to my fingers and feet, which are stinging and throbbing so agonisingly that I can only yelp. The fingers feel as though they are about to burst. I beat my hands fiercely on my knees to help get the blood circulating, but can't do anything about my feet except curse and curse. I've no idea where we are, and don't care. We continue to fly unevenly southwards for several minutes, and gradually I return to normal, except for the ache and humming in my ears, which I know will persist for several hours. These are the penalties for coming down so quickly.

I look below and see a town. It is Roulers, that nest of Hun aerodromes. But there are no Huns about in the sky, though we see several of our formations. Pratt does not attempt to get back to the 20,000 feet level, but we mount gradually to 15,000 while searching for somebody to fight in between the topmost masses of cloud. We are archied indifferently four times. Then our two hours are up, Pratt turns westwards, and gives the washout at 10,000 over Ypres.

We follow him down to our aerodrome at La Gorgue. The intense cold from our highest flying still persists in my body, especially in my hands and feet, but I begin to unfreeze when we reach 3,000. From then on I am no longer cold, and ten minutes later, as I climb down from my machine to a sweltering tarmac, I am perspiring uncomfortably. And save for the singing and deafness in my ears, that brief journey into the vault of heaven, that very trying spell at 20,000, that alarming moment of faintness, that agonising descent—all are forgotten as we hasten to scrape off most of the whale grease and discard our sweaters and gloves and thigh-boots and flying coats and all the rest of our high-flying open cockpit paraphernalia.

FIVE

SCARED!

It was after about a dozen patrols in May and June 1917, during which I had been quickly initiated into the tricky business of fighting Albatros D–IIIs, and had with incredible luck managed not to be shot down, though not without some nerve-racking escapes, that I had an aerial skirmish which gave me a welcome new outlook on life.

I remember this episode not because of its conclusive result but because of the lack of one. There were more exciting, more dramatic and more victorious patrols, with German aeroplanes shot down or my own sprayed with bullets, that I recall more vividly, but this particular affair made its mark because it was a significant turning point in my build-up as a fighter pilot.

We were on a morning patrol of four some ten miles inside German territory, under a sky of watery blue, half-filled with banks of soft cloud, the sort of weather for ambush. After half an hour at 14,000 feet without sign of an enemy, we spotted four Albatroses coming towards us from the east, about a thousand feet below. They obviously did not see us, and our leader was able to wheel behind them before diving. I put my sight on the right rear Hun of the formation, and when our leader fired at 150 yards range, and I pressed the trigger, my target broke away, turned steeply, and a loose dogfight began.

None of them appeared to be hit, and we sorted out our opponents with now the expectation of facing an unpleasant time as the consequence of our poor shooting in the initial dive. I quickly got on to the tail of the first D–III that came across my front and gave him a burst of ten rounds. He at once pulled off in a curve to a flank, and I followed, making sure by a backwards glance that another Hun wasn't behind me.

As I turned steeply after him I fired a second burst, but it was a difficult deflection shot, and the tracer sped well off the mark between his port wings. But before I could aim another burst, he abruptly dipped his nose and dived away. I went after him, firing continuously, but he soon left me behind, and I watched him level out about 1,500 feet below me and then set off eastwards. As I also levelled out I thought, Why has he packed up? I could hardly have hit him, for my shooting was wild, and no tracer had gone near either pilot or engine. If he'd had a gun jam he would surely have climbed up above me, as Albatroses usually did, while he rectified it. And he could hardly have run out of ammunition, for his friends, who'd presumably done a similar amount of shooting before meeting us, were still firing briskly up above.

As I climbed steeply to rejoin the fight, I suddenly realised the obvious. Good lord, I thought, he was scared! He ran away!

It came to me as a surprising revelation. In every fight I'd had so far it was I who was scared in some degree. I'd escaped by a miracle when alone and attacked by six D–IIIs. I'd been badly shot up three or four times. I'd come to realise that the Pup was no match for the Albatros other than at great heights, and except for its life-saving manœuvrability I had little faith in it as a fighting machine, nor in my slow-firing Vickers gun with its frequent stoppages.

Because the Albatros was so much more lethal a fighter than the Pup, able to dominate almost every encounter with its greater speed, climb and fire-power, and so conferring on its pilot the advantage of the initiative, I'd come to think that they were all supermen, of the calibre of Richtofen, crack shots and pilots, confident, ruthless and without fear. It had never occurred to me that they might sometimes be scared.

But by this one incident I saw that the occupants of those intimidating Albatroses were human, could experience the same moments
of funk that I had done. Certainly this pilot might have been very
young, could have been in his first fight, could have panicked when
he saw tracer flashing past his head, for when one is new to fear it is
easy to panic, to want to flee. But whatever the reason, he had been
scared.

And from that moment my attitude to the enemy changed. Maybe
the Albatros *was* a better plane than the Pup, but the men in them
counted too. Why shouldn't I as a pilot be as good as, or even better
than, the pilot of an Albatros, or any other Hun fighter? He could
quite easily be quaking in his boots at meeting a Pup which he'd
know could make rings round him, especially at high altitudes. The
very thought of it gave me a specific stiffening of courage. I was still
sometimes in a cold sweat when I went into a fight, but it didn't last
long or worry me greatly.

From now on such spasms of real cold feet as I experienced arose
chiefly from awareness of the technical superiority of the Albatros.
And in these disquietudes I was not alone. The most common cause
of serious strain among a large proportion of the Royal Flying Corps
in 1916–17 was simply that they were mounted on planes much less
efficient than those of their opponents. This was frustrating enough
for the pilots of fighters such as Pups and Nieuports, but we could at
least fight, and with luck and skill hold our own, but those who flew
such outdated craft as Sopwith and Nieuport two-seaters, or such
utterly bad ones as B.E.s and R.E.s, could neither fight effectively
nor escape.

Even the pilot of a Pup soon discovered that if he were to survive
he must temper boldness with caution. To be reckless or even too
brave could quickly be fatal. A man might be of truly heroic mould,
but in a Pup he would only die more speedily. As for the two-seaters,
discretion was the better part of valour, their only sure recourse was
to start running away well before the Hun dived.

We were often cynically amused at the falseness of the image of the R.F.C. which was held by the public in England. Certainly we were of a special breed, for we actually enjoyed flying at a time when to fly was considered both dangerous and slightly mad. Certainly we were mostly carefree, reckless, and even madcap, for these were exactly the qualities that prompted young men to turn to flying, but we were far from being the impossible creatures created by the newspapers. That we were all intrepid, daredevil, hell-bent birdmen. That we never leapt into the air except to flirt with death. That we never had wind-up, in fact didn't know what fear was, that we attacked whatever the odds, and got our Hun always in a five-shot burst, and if at last we were unluckily hit we dived to our glorious finish with a devil-may-care smile, defiant to the end.

It would have been nice had things been even remotely like that, but the fact was that most of us who flew in France were scared a little, and sometimes a lot, almost every time we went into action. And this covered not only fighter dog-fights but encounters with and by two-seaters, being badly archied, and, not least, repeated trench-strafing. Yet although we may have often flinched from our jobs, we did them to the best of our will-power and our nerves.

These qualities naturally varied from man to man, and to even the dullest of us it became clear that in the matter of fear and courage we were all made differently. Some pilots and observers, not a very large proportion, really did not know the meaning of fear. They were men of steel. Their minds never dwelt on their risks, never considered what might happen to them. Maybe they had no imagination. To them, air fighting was a sport. This was how Richtofen regarded it— until he was wounded, when his attitude changed. And such aces as Bishop, McCudden, Collishaw, MacLaren, Nungesser, McKeever, and the American, Luke, ruthless killers all, apparently never knew a twinge of fear in even their most desperate exploits.

But other aces were different, such as Ball, who came close to a breakdown halfway through his fighting career, and Mannock, tormented by his obsession of being shot down in flames, and Guynemer, who became just a bundle of nerves. These men forced themselves to reject their fears, to go on, to show no hesitation in attacking the enemy on sight. And alongside them were many hundreds of other pilots and observers who every day, maybe three or four times a day, had to will themselves to fight.

Our dreads were common to us all. We were not greatly afraid of being killed, indeed we seldom consciously thought of it, for we were young, and those who have not had time to taste life to the full place no great value on it. And so we were not actively worried at the possibility of being snuffed out by a bullet or blown to smithereens by archie. These were sharp and sudden ends. What we *were* scared of, most of us, was being set on fire or having the plane break up, either through enemy bullets smashing the fragile structure or by collision in a frantic dog-fight. From these plights there was no possible escape because we had no parachutes.

It is understandable why even the bravest had an abiding horror of being burnt alive. Many fighter pilots, though unmoved at the sight of an enemy plane crashing into a funeral pyre, or disintegrating into fragments in the air, were disturbed when they sent one down in flames. Even that hardened killer, Richtofen, eventually came to find a distaste in doing it. Yet some top-scorers, such as the relentless Bishop, were satisfied to see their victims alight, for there was then no argument, theirs was the indisputable victory, seen by everyone.

It was usual to find that the inner fears which held so many of us vanished in the actual business of air fighting. In my own narrow experience I came to realise that during a dog-fight or even in attack on two-seaters I was excited rather than alarmed, though before the attack opened, especially against other fighters, there was always a quickened pulse, a tingling of the skin, a trembling, even sweating. And afterwards you might reflect uneasily on your close shaves, but your misgivings were hidden. No one ever talked about his secret dreads. Only obliquely, in gruesome jokes and ante-room ditties, was the spectre of fear admitted, and then but to be mockingly dismissed.

After the war I occasionally read accounts of air fighting in 1917 and 1918 which told of pilots, and not only of single-seater fighters, who habitually carried into the air a flask of brandy or whisky from which they took generous swigs whenever combat loomed. This may well have happened, though I could more readily imagine them doing this to keep out the cold at high altitudes, but so far as my experience went, I never once heard of a pilot relying on dutch courage, for even the most unthinking would realise that the reaction would impair both flying and shooting.

The resolution needed by the airmen of World War I was of a special kind, and it was demanded from the moment you began to learn to fly. This process, with the uncertain methods of instruction of 1916–17, was so crowded with lethal crashes that nearly as many lives were lost in training schools in England as in the warring skies of France. Indeed so reluctant were some pupils to face the probability every time they left the ground of smashing themselves up through ignorant handling of the controls that they declined to carry on. One gunner captain, whom I well remember at Netheravon in 1916, threw in his hand, declared himself a coward, and went back to his battery. Yet a few months later, when I ran across him in London, he wore the ribbon of the D.S.O. He was a proven man of valour, but not of the kind peculiar to the airman.

On active service the differences between the brands of courage required in the air and on the ground were even more marked. The infantryman needed superhuman fortitude merely to exist in water-logged trenches, with rats and lice and frost-bite and rotting corpses as his daily lot, but he needed also a brave heart to endure the incessant risk from bullets and shell-fire, and even more the murderous carnage of an attack, when he and his comrades might be mown down by the thousand, falling like swaths of grass before the scythe.

But his courage, his will to fight, was sustained by the physical presence of his fellows, by his loyalty to them and theirs to him. He had the morale-supporting knowledge that vast numbers were facing dangers identical to his. He was stiffened by discipline, which conditioned him to go forward to almost certain death when every instinct told him to flee. And if he survived long spells of exposure and hazard, and saw most of his comrades go under, he could still keep going because he then sank into a kind of numb fatalism.

The airman's work was physically immeasurably easier, but it did demand a particular order of courage, and especially from the fighter pilot, whose job was to seek combat and not to avoid it, as reconnaissance and artillery spotting planes had perforce to try to do. The pilot of a twin- or multi-seater had the sustaining companionship of his crew, but the fighter pilot was alone. Even if he started a fight as a member of a formation, when it developed it became usually a matter of single combat. He fought not shoulder to shoulder with thousands of others but as an individual in a glove-tight aeroplane miles up in the sky, and in a dog-fight, during a desperately contested duel, he could easily feel that he was fighting the war by himself.

To be able to fight on his own was the distinguishing mark of the fighter pilot, but with it he had to be imbued with the aggressive spirit. He had to hunt for battle, and several times a day, several times an hour, might have to pass through spells of intensely lethal fighting, with split-second margins between life and death, that left him emotionally and physically spent.

And he was but human. The stock of courage which a man possesses is expendable, and he loses a little of it every time he runs a razor's edge risk. The strain is deepened if his weapon is inferior and he knows he is at a disadvantage even before the fight starts. That is when the most valiant man can reach the stage when his nerve begins to falter, when he realises he is becoming scared. Yet even if he were not a natural fire-eater and danger lover, and whether a fighter pilot or the occupant of an indifferent two-seater, he seldom failed to live with his tensions and fears, to master them, and to carry out his duties properly. But to know that the enemy, in spite of his better equipment, had his tensions and fears too, could be a refreshing fillip to morale.

That in 1916 and most of 1917, except for a brief interlude when the Fokker monoplane was mastered, the Germans' superior aeroplanes gave them assurance and extra courage, while the mostly mediocre British machines, with their background of heavy casualties, diluted both skill and resolution, was strikingly evidenced when squadrons, my own among them, were re-equipped in the second half of 1917 with new type winners such as Camels, SE5s and Bristols.

We were then all inspired with a thrusting belligerence that quickly robbed the German fighter pilots of the advantages and initiative they had enjoyed for so long. It was from then on that the gall and wormwood of air combat, and the handicap of being more or less scared half the time, was largely transferred to our German opponents.

SIX

DAWN PATROL

'Quarter to four, sir. You're on patrol in half an hour. And it's a fine morning.'

The orderly batman, himself called by the night guard five minutes earlier, shakes me gently, and speaks in a murmur so as not to disturb the other pilots asleep in the hut.

I tumble from my bed and sit on it, yawning, and feeling more than sluggish after a generous intake of alcohol the evening before. The batman treads silently in his rubber-soled shoes to the opposite corner and stirs out Courtneidge, who is also on the dawn patrol. Satisfied that we are both well awake, he then steals out, carefully closing the door behind him, and creeps on to his next port of call. No clumsy footsteps, no early-morning cheerfulness, no whistling, for everyone else is asleep, and he knows they prefer to stay that way.

It is practically dark, and I can scarcely see what I am doing, but don't like to switch on my torch for fear of waking the two lucky types snoring peacefully in their corners. I dress dazedly, fumbling for my clothes, trying to make no noise. Where the hell did I put my second sweater, my long woolly scarf? Damn, I nearly knocked the blasted table over! Who the devil's moved my helmet and gloves? And so on. Whispered curses coming from the dimness of Court-neidge's corner proclaim that he's having his troubles too.

But in three minutes we are dressed. No time for brushing teeth, no time even for washing, except to wipe my face with a damp sponge. Courtneidge comes across, we leave the hut together. I close the door noiselessly behind me—not that I am excessively considerate by nature, but I am well aware that if I don't play fair, the two sleepers, when their turn for the dawn job comes, will make sure that I am wide awake with them.

As we make for the Mess in the near darkness, we are joined by two other muffled figures, Joske and Odell. We grunt our good mornings, but say nothing else. As we move along, I momentarily shiver, for the air is chilly after the rain, but it is sweet and fragrant, and the damp ground smells of the richness of the soil.

In the Mess the orderly cook, also called by the night guard, has prepared a snack breakfast of tea, hard-boiled eggs, bread and margarine. He puts everything before us without a word. We don't speak either—this is no hour for light chat. We gulp the food down not because we're hungry but because we have to have it inside us, for nobody can fly and fight on an empty stomach. When we come down from patrol we shall have our real breakfast at leisure, porridge, maybe coffee, maybe bacon and sausage and marmalade. Something to look forward to.

We light cigarettes, then, with scarcely a word between us, leave the Mess, wrap our scarves round our necks, for it is still sharp and shivery, and clamber into the waiting Crossley, engine quietly running. There is now a faint steely light—we can see the other huts and the farm alongside which our encampment is scattered.

Five minutes later we are by the hangars at the further side of the aerodrome. Here the mechanics, also pulled from their beds by the ubiquitous night guard, have drawn out our respective Pups, started the engines, and run them up for us. We utter our good mornings morosely to the sergeant and the fitters and riggers and armourers, who regard us bleakly as though it is our fault that they are here at this absurd hour.

The air no longer has the scent of rain, but only of burnt castor oil from the Le Rhône rotary engines. In the flight office, our somnolence dispelled, we don our flying gear while Joske, our leader, gives his instructions. We're on a Line Patrol, but we shall go five or ten miles over, he tells us, and for Christ's sake keep a sharp look-out eastwards when the sun comes up. He doesn't need to tell us, we know what can happen if the Hun comes at you out of a dazzling yellow sunrise.

A light mist hovers low over the aerodrome, but it is not sufficiently dense to bother us. The air is completely still and we need a long run to take off. We leave the ground in quick succession, and join up in formation overhead, and although by now daylight is flooding the empty vault of the sky above, lower down it is still dark enough for us to seek guidance from the flames of each other's exhausts.

As we lift over the sleeping countryside, everything seems snug, rural, tranquil, utterly remote from the notion of war. The pale grey mist still lingers over the low-lying ground, but now, as the world begins to waken and show signs of life, it is mingled with splashes of blue smoke rising from camp-fire and cottages. We pass over a village and the smoke from its chimneys clings to the houses, enveloping them in a ghostly blue veil. It seems incredible that on so peaceful a summer's morning we are riding into the skies to kill other flyers also taking wing into the dawn.

Climbing steadily southwards, we quickly meet the light mounting from the east. At first, a pale yellow flush that marks the dark edge of the earth, then, as the minutes pass, that turns to a pinkish gold. The first diffused rays of the sun, which still hides below the horizon, pierce the steely sky and transform it to pale blue. Below lies Hunland, but I can see nothing of it, for the mist is there too, and the ground is blanketed.

We are not the only early birds. Silhouetted blackly against the eastern glow hangs the motionless sausage-shape of an observation balloon, and the line of them stretching north and south is easily picked up. When we pass over them and look back, they shine yellow in the sun's light. Soon, as we turn eastwards we shall see the line of dark silhouetted enemy balloons some five miles beyond the trenches.

At 8,000 feet we are alone except for a couple of B.E.2e's beneath us, creeping along their artillery spotting beats. Far below them a double line of spasmodic red flashes, the bursting of British and German shells, marks the course of the opposing trench systems. We move eastwards over the hell that lies there, and on into Hunland. As we enter the archie belt, our practised leader begins a series of gentle, erratic changes of course, and just in time, for archie, with no other customers, gives us his full attention, and at once sends up a sighting salvo.

But our zigzagging has deceived him, and the four black woolly balls, each centred with its red flash, though good for height are over a hundred yards to our right. We hear the quick wuff! wuff! wuff! wuff! plainly enough, but they are much too far away to worry us. Archie is angry, and sends up three more salvos in rapid succession, each one nearer to us than the last. But we are moving eastwards at ninety miles an hour, and as we draw out of his effective range, we hear more bursts behind us, and know that he will now give it up, and allow us to enter Hunland without further trouble.

Mounting smoothly into the sky and the light, and being welcomed not over-warmly by archie, I find that yesterday's cobwebs are quickly vanishing. My spirits rise. The smooth roar of my willing engine is the voice of our challenge to the Huns—come up and meet us, it seems to shout, and join us in a friendly morning scrap!

We look eastwards to greet the sun as its golden rim edges above the horizon. We are seeing it long before the earthbound mortals below, but soon, as it rises higher and its flame floods the eastern sky, it becomes our enemy, for in its dazzle the enemy may be hiding. We cannot see into it, nor can we see downwards towards the earth, for the bright light above gives substance to the early haze, and hides everything from us.

But westwards all is clear. In the distance are groups of small woolly clouds, soon turning to gold as the glinting rays touch them. They look quaintly like flocks of sheep suspended in the sky. They are the forerunners of other clouds, larger, big banks of cumulus looming high behind.

Now full daylight is upon us. The void of the heavens is a deeper blue. We are at 12,000 feet, well inside Hunland. Surely by now some enemy formation is up, looking for prey with all the advantages on their side? I put a thumb close to my left eye to mask the sun, and gaze intently into the golden glow around it. No glittering specks there, so far as I can see.

Abruptly, I am alerted by the sound of shots, but it is only Joske firing a dozen rounds to make sure his gun is working. We spread out and follow his example, firing casually into Hunland. Always I wonder what happens to the bullets when they reach the ground— they are just as likely to hit a Frenchman as a German. Then we close in again to formation. Not that we are in really close formation, there is no need for that, but we're close enough for Joske to be able to twist round and gesture to us and give signals.

Watching out for Huns while going eastwards is not a burden, for at least one's potential troubles are ahead, but when at last we swing southwards, we must then be continuously searching to our left to guard the flank. The same again, but on the other side, when we reach the end of our beat and turn round to the north. But all this is of secondary consequence compared with when we turn westwards, and present our tails towards the sun, for then every one of us must strain his neck to look constantly behind—and not just to glance behind, but stare intently, examining every sector in turn, especially above, for nothing can be more unhealthy than to be caught unawares by a Hun formation diving out of the sun. And of the four of us, it is Odell, at the rear position of our diamond formation, who has the worst job, for if we *are* jumped, he will get shot at first. Naturally he knows this and takes even more interest in his tail than the rest of us.

Looking downwards, I see that under the warmth of the swiftly rising sun, the haze and mist are being put to rout. A strong westerly wind has sprung up, shown by long tails of smoke from towns below us, in German hands. Another enemy, this westerly wind, always carrying us deeper into Hunland.

Until now we have had no excitement whatever. The four of us have patrolled our beat, some five to ten miles in Hunland, at half-throttle, and seemingly scarcely moving at all, as there are no nearby clouds to show up our speed. We are now at 15,000, have been up an hour and have seen no aeroplanes other than the B.E.s at 6,000 feet, so Joske decides to look for trouble further into Hun territory, and we climb eastwards. The sky is clear, and the sun is still low enough to be a menace, but not nearly so much as during that first hour.

As we swing eastwards in a wide sweep, I suddenly see five specks a little below us coming from the north-east. They are not easy to pick out against the distant patchwork earth below, and in case Joske has not seen them, I dive in front of him, rock my wings and point down. He at once finds them, lifts a gauntleted hand in acknowledgement, and rocks his wings to warn the others. The two formations are approaching each other, the space between us is closing rapidly. Joske is still climbing to gain extra height. They are V-strutters—I recognise them as D–IIIs—there is no mistaking their sleek pigeon-breasted curve. They see us and surprisingly turn sharply south.

Joske rocks his wings again and drops into a shallow dive with engine full on. We are four, they five, but we have height, and if only we get close enough we shall smash them on the dive. I am sweating with excitement, my finger is on the trigger, my Aldis is lined on the left winger, green and white, as I watch for Joske's tracer to flash away.

Then suddenly, just as we open fire, the Huns swing sharply to the west and come directly under us. Joske steepens our dive, but we can't get our sights on to them as they race beneath us, a hundred yards below. We swirl round madly, and there they are, plunging away to the northwards. We drop into vertical dives after them, engines full on, firing wildly at 300 yards' range, but it is hopeless, they gradually draw away from us. Not for the first time, we apppreciate that the Albatros D–III is twenty-five miles an hour faster than the Pup.

I can't understand why they have refused combat, for in a dogfight, even at 15,000, five D–IIIs, each with two fast-firing Spandaus compared with the Pup's single, slow-firing Vickers, plus their quicker climb and speed, could have made mincemeat of us. Afterwards, in the squadron office, we decided that they must have been four new boys being shown round the Lines by an experienced hand. *He* knew exactly what to do, but in a free-for-all the others would have been easy victims for us.

In chasing them we have dived down to 8,000, and Joske levels out while we take up position behind him. And as we do so, there is the sharp rattle of gun-fire, and tracers flash among us. We whip round and I turn steeply to the right, the Pup's best trick to avoid giving the Hun a target. I see them swirling above us, still masked by the low eastern sun out of which they have attacked us. They are D–IIIs. We have been caught napping! And in a clear sky!

At first I cannot see how many there are and I don't really care, all I'm thinking about is avoiding being hit. Tracers whizz past me, alongside, to port, to starboard, above, below. I seem to be enveloped in them, but miraculously none hits me. I know it can be fatal to swerve to change direction, for if I bank from one turn to the other I offer an instant's sitting target, so I continue my steep turning to the right, meanwhile out of the corner of my eye trying to get my bearings and spot my attacker.

Tracers flash by again, and the crackle of bullets is so close that I cringe into my cockpit. But the D–III can't turn as tightly as I can, can't get his guns on to me. Another D–III speeds at an angle across my front, turning away. I glimpse the curving underside, the pale blue wings, the black cross on the fin. He is about a hundred yards away. Instinctively I turn after him, still in a steep turn, and at once find his tail and fin in the ring sight.

I press the trigger, the tracers jump out towards him, enter his fuselage halfway up, I edge them towards the pilot—then *crack-ak-ak* behind me, I jerk the stick back into my belly, the Pup suddenly kicks sharply and dips down—I have flown into the blue Hun's slipstream. But my attacker is thrown off and I level out, still on a turn. The blue Hun has gone, but another is firing at me from three-quarters astern, much too accurately, the tracers slip between the wings to port, two yards from me. I kick the rudder and skid clear. I think, Christ, I'll never get out of this, I've not had time to draw breath yet.

Dazedly I glimpse other machines banking round me, but I don't have time to count. A mottled Hun comes across my front firing at a Pup. I swing after him, give him a deflection shot, twenty rounds, the tracers seem to go right into the engine, he lifts suddenly and climbs away. I try to follow, the Pup hangs on the prop, but just can't climb any steeper.

Suddenly the general crackle of guns increases. But the Albatroses are pulling away. I see them now—only four. And I see why they're bolting. A trio of F.E.2b's has spotted the fight and come wading in, their gunners hosing the Hun with long streams of tracer. God, I think, what guts these chaps have got, to join in a dog-fight in such antiquated tubs as those birdcage pushers. But they do the trick, the D–IIIs vanish to the east.

I take a deep breath and flop back in my seat. I'm feeling somewhat sick. It all started so suddenly, I had no time to think, and never really knew what was happening. I'd made certain we were done for. At 8,000 the Pup is completely outclassed by the Albatros. You can't get away, you've got to fight it out—with one gun against two.

We circle close around the F.E.s and wave our thanks. The pilots and observers wave back, then join up and pass on westwards. Obviously they were on the homeward run from a reconnaissance when they saw our scrap. I don't envy them sitting there exposed to the full blast of air, especially the observer—open cockpit is the word! Far worse than for us. None of the Pups is adrift, and we resume formation and carry on with the patrol. But we'd been lucky. We had allowed ourselves to be taken by surprise, out of the early-morning sun, where danger always lies and only the marvellous manœuvrability of our faithful Pups, plus the intervention of the F.E.s, had saved us from a bad mauling.

We still have half an hour's patrol to do, and Joske resumes our beat up and down the Lines. Within two minutes, Odell gives the distress signal and glides away westwards. His engine has been damaged, as we learn afterwards. We also learn that we have all taken punishment, but one has been hit in a vital spot.

By now the sky has changed, for the flocks of sheep have come

Above: Bristol Fighter F.2B
with Sunbeam Arab engine
Right: Camel of 61
Squadron, 110 Le Rhône
engine, under inspection by
Air Commodore T. C. R.
Higgins, 1918
Below: S.E.5a of 85
Squadron *(Imperial War
Museum)*

swiftly in from the westwards, and have already passed underneath, followed by larger masses of cumulus, whose white billowing tops slide along not far below us. We see no more Huns, and Joske, feeling in a good mood, keeps us skimming close to the solid-looking mountains of woolly cloud. As we swing round their swelling hills and valleys, I realise that not a trace of the dawn hangover remains.

Suddenly I see by the dashboard watch that it is half past six. We've been up over two hours, and because of the fight and the cloud-hopping, I've not noticed it. But now that the job is practically finished, I realise that I'm famished, and my thoughts turn to the bacon and sausage awaiting me. At this moment, Joske gives the washout signal, and we break up and make our separate ways home. Another dawn patrol is over.

SEVEN

DOWN TO EARTH

Dusk was turning to darkness as I touched down alongside the lake at Dickebusch, south-west of Ypres, and I was lucky to manage a landing of sorts in the hundred yards or so that lay between the eastern side of the lake and the rear of a line of field guns in action.

The reason I'd had to come down was that, after losing my companion on this, my first late-evening patrol, then vainly searching for him to the north of Ypres, then falling into a surprise encounter with a Hun two-seater, whose observer managed to graze my leg in a brief exchange of shots, I realised it was now too late to reach the aerodrome at La Gorgue before darkness fell.

I had to get down to the nearest bit of friendly earth as soon as possible, and I dived west, losing height quickly. In the deepening gloom below, Dickebusch Lake was the only landmark that I recognised with certainty as being on our side of the Lines, and so I alighted close to it, and also practically among the guns. The battery had begun the routine evening hate, but the gunners stopped the war for a few minutes to help me from the machine, which had tipped on its nose in a shell-hole, and give me a whisky and a field-dressing, together with a tin helmet, for the Huns had started their evening hate too, and shrapnel was in the air.

The officers of the battery gave me quite a welcome, though because this was my first close-quarters plunge into the war on the ground, I was in a haze trying to explain to the major why I'd called on him so unexpectedly, and at the same time adjust myself to the sudden transition from a quiet gliding aeroplane to the shattering din of a field battery shelling and being shelled.

For the German gunners, after plastering Dickebusch village, now switched to us, and we began what was for me an anxious five minutes before the fire moved on to harass somebody else. Shells were exploding all around me, so it seemed, and one fell with a heart-stopping *crr—rr—umpp!* about thirty yards away, but as none of the gunners took any more notice of this burst than the others, I put on as brave a front as I could manage. This was my first taste of being under shell-fire, other than by archie in the air, and I decided there and then that I wouldn't want it regularly.

The battery was despatching salvos every minute or so, and though the sharp crack of the detonations was uncomfortable, so that I was glad to wear the eardrums that someone handed to me, it was thrilling to be with the guns in action, to see the dark moving figures of the gunners silhouetted against the flashes of flame and the smoke. Eastwards, where the trenches lay, the front line troops, British and German, were sending up star-shells, green and white flares, Very lights and all kinds of other fireworks. It was weird to watch, and I was fascinated to learn that it went on every night.

While I was still trying vainly to put up with the shelling without flinching every few seconds, the whole area suddenly started blaring with klaxon gas-alarms. Somebody thoughtfully gave me a box respirator, and I needed it, for gas-shells went on dropping for over two hours. They plopped down with a modest burst and a phutt! of gas, which, as there was no wind, hung around on the ground instead of dispersing like smoke, and this meant that respirators had to be worn long after the gas-shells stopped falling. When they did, high explosive began again, which annoyed the major, as he could see no reason for any break with routine.

Some time after I landed, when I'd gathered my wits, I asked the battery signals officer to send a message to my squadron, pinpointing my position and asking that the machine be salvaged, as it was but little damaged, and lay over a mile from the front.

About eleven, there was a lull in the shelling, and, feeling weary, I sat against the sandbagged wall of an emplacement, still wearing my flying gear and respirator, topped by the helmet. Amazingly, in spite of the resumption of the shelling, I dropped off to sleep, and sat there until daybreak. When I woke, everything was quiet. I heard blackbirds calling, and saw water-fowl skimming across the lake. How they survived in this inferno of gas and shelling was a mystery.

I stood up and looked around. It was a fine morning, with clear sky, and our balloons were already up, one nearly overhead. My Pup was covered with camouflage netting. I realised now that the battery, like the others on our flanks, was sited below a slope, which, as the major later explained, hid it from the enemy on the Messines and Whytschaete ridge. Suddenly a whistle shrilled, and a loud voice cried 'Still, everybody!' To my surprise, I saw that all the gunners had frozen into immobility, and so I froze too. A minute later the whistle blew again, and we all relaxed. I found that the reason for this display, which was repeated several times during the day, was a German reconnaissance plane flying over us at about 15,000 feet. The gunners had an abiding worry that enemy aeroplanes could pinpoint their position, and until the one overhead had passed on, everyone stood motionless, not even looking up, for faces would show as white blobs.

The major told me this while I took a breakfast of baked beans on toast with him in his dugout, a curve of corrugated iron protected by sandbags, and here he told me that during last evening's strafe one of his gunners had been killed and three wounded. Halfway through the morning he took me on a routine visit to an observation post just over the crest of the slope. I left my flying gear, except the sheepskin boots, which I had to wear, in the dugout, as the day was already warm.

The post was in what was left of a cottage, and had a clear view across the shell-pitted ground to the Lines and beyond into Hunland. I watched the battery do a shoot on to the remains of a biggish building a few hundred yards on the further side of the belts of rusty barbed wire that denoted no-man's-land.

The major then asked if I'd like to visit the front line, an offer I leapt at, and off we went, at first alongside a zigzagging communication trench. Suddenly, in a magical sort of way, spurts of dust started jumping up in the soft earth some twenty yards to our front, and I heard the distant stutter of a machine-gun. The major called 'Quick'! and dropped into the trench, and I followed so smartly I almost reached the duckboards first.

We continued our now much slower way under cover until we came to a maze which I gathered was part of the reserve trench system, and here we surfaced in the skeleton of the village of Voormezeele. A handful of troops were there, doing nothing in particular, except for a couple who were shovelling out a shallow grave for what I suddenly realised was the corpse of a Tommy, his head covered with a sandbag. They explained that he'd been caught by a stray shell-burst an hour earlier.

At this moment there came a remote rattle of machine-gun fire from high above. About 10,000 feet up to the eastwards, a flock of aeroplanes was milling around in a dog-fight. This was very interesting to me, as I'd never previously seen an air fight from the ground, but I wasn't the only one interested, for the two Tommies stopped digging, and, like the other men there, gazed aloft intently. The major later told me that everybody stopped whatever he was doing, short of hand-to-hand combat, to watch a scrap in the air, and usually to lay bets on the result.

The machines, too far distant for me to identify them, still swirled round each other, firing in short bursts. Then one went down steeply, with another on his tail, gun going. Suddenly the wings folded back, and he went into a twisting vertical dive. The pursuer zoomed up and rejoined the scrap. Soon another plane went down in a spin, then the fight petered out, and the machines drew away, east and west.

As the Tommies resumed their digging, one exclaimed, 'Catch me in one of them bloody contraptions!' They hadn't noticed that I was a pilot. The major grinned, and beckoned me to continue our walk. We tramped on for what seemed hours along more zigzagging trenches until we came to the support line, from which we went to the front line. He said we were now in the village of St Eloi, but there was nothing but heaps of rubble. We passed through traverses, topped neatly with sandbags, and lined with troops sitting casually about, and looking very bored. Soon we turned off into a narrow kinked trench leading to the advanced posts, and here some of the troops were at the ready, leaning up against the parapets, keeping look-out through small gaps.

Everything seemed peaceful enough, though to me it was incredible that 500 miles of fortified trenches like this one stretched from the Channel to Switzerland, and every yard was guarded day and night by armed soldiery, British, French and German, watching unceasingly through loopholes.

The idea of squatting in a trench waiting to be killed by a random bullet, or by a shell sent by an invisible enemy miles away, or by hidden machine-guns while struggling through the wire in an over-the-top attack, didn't appeal to me in the least. After all, in an aeroplane you saw the man you were fighting, you matched your skill and guts against his, you both put up a fight, and maybe you won or maybe you lost or maybe you ran away for another day. But it was a fight. And even archie, perhaps a whole battery, could be avoided. But in the fighting on the ground, chance played too big a part, being shelled and machine-gunned wasn't fighting at all, but just indiscriminate slaughter.

I mounted the fire-step and peered through a periscope, but saw little more than entangled barbed wire. A friendly captain invited me to have a go with a machine-gun, so I mounted another step and fired 200 rounds over the wire at a blockhouse on the Boche slope opposite. This gave me an enormous kick, especially when they started answering back, and I heard the crack of bullets over my head, and the whine of ricochets.

We returned to the battery by a different route, partly through the skeleton of a wood in a dip in the ground, where we were able to leave the trench. I was trudging alongside the major when he suddenly cried 'Dive!' and jumped into a convenient shell-hole, and again I followed excessively quickly. Immediately there was a hellish explosion about twenty yards away. We waited, cowering in the hole, and another five explosions followed, all further west. The major, as we stood up and dusted ourselves, said in a matter-of-fact way that they were whizz-bangs, which you can hear coming a few seconds away, and this gives you time to dive for cover.

It was nice to know this, but I realised more clearly than ever that this frequent, nerve-racking ritual of jumping into holes just to keep alive made no great appeal to me. When we got home from our four-mile stroll, the major was perfectly fresh, but I, what with the heat, the dust, the diving into holes and the sheepskin boots, was flogged, and said so, whereupon he produced two bottles of Bass from his slender store.

During the rest of the day there was much activity in the air, though I saw no more Huns. I spotted a formation of ten Pups going north-east, very high, and later two Pups came along at about 10,000, then wheeled eastwards. Afterwards I found they were from 46 Squadron, McDonald and Caudwell, and the latter was wounded in a scrap a quarter of an hour later. I also saw B.E.s and R.E.s doing shoots, and formations of Nieuports, Spads, F.E.2d's and Sopwith two-seaters, a flight of the new Bristols, and several small groups of Sopwith Triplanes, which belong to the R.N.A.S. It was most intriguing to get this view of our planes patrolling up and down at different heights east of the lines, something we can't see from our aerodromes, while in the air we only see what's going on just around us.

In the evening I went to the major's dugout for a dinner of sardines, followed by stew, adorned by another Bass. The evening hate was well on, and the Boche kept up his bombardment for over an hour, during which time the major's portable gramophone never stopped. I can't say that I was greatly interested in music, as the shells seemed to creep closer all the time. One burst with a shattering roar practically on top of us, so it seemed to me, which made me sweat with fright, but the major merely put on another record. Next morning I inspected the hole, ten yards from the dugout, and big enough to bury a cow in.

Although I didn't much relish this sort of thing, to look out from the shelter of the dugout and see the vivid flashes of the guns ten paces away, and hear the sharp crack of the explosions, the crash of bursting Boche shells, the whine of shrapnel, all made a memorable experience for me. But not for the major, who kept the gramophone grinding on. I told him that what I disliked about being shelled was not knowing whether the next one might land on your head, but his reply was that if that happened I'd know not a thing about it.

'Better than being shot down in an aeroplane,' he said. 'I wouldn't be one of you flying chaps for all the tea in China.' And one of his subalterns, who had joined us, agreed. Both said that nothing would induce them to fly. They'd seen too many planes come down with their wings off or in flames, and the occupants often jumping out. 'Why don't you have parachutes, like the balloonists?' they asked, and that was a question to which I had no answer.

After a while we were joined by two infantry lieutenants who were on liaison with the battery, and who were greatly interested in me and the Flying Corps and its peculiar ways. We talked of the contrasts between air and ground, and compared the life of R.F.C. flyers, doing highly lethal jobs two or three times a day but with a safe and comfortable home to go to, with the dreary round of the Poor Bloody Infantry—front line, support, reserve, rest in some cheerless village, then front line again, there to be shot at day and night by every kind of missile, with over-the-top massacres to break the monotony, while enduring mud, rats, lice, frost-bite, trench feet and the stench of rotting corpses. Yet, like the gunners, who were shelled even more often than the P.B.I., they preferred it all as a lesser evil to flying and being shot down in flames.

I was surprised to learn that they knew all about Richtofen, though they only spoke of him as the Red Baron. From what they said he seemed to be around every day, shooting down our two-seaters as he liked, and I concluded that any Albatros with red paint on it was reckoned to be piloted by the Baron. To me it was extraordinary that he was the only airmen they had any knowledge of, for they couldn't name a single British flyer except Albert Ball, and the legendary Mad Major, who they said often flew low and looped over the Boche trenches and behaved in a thoroughly mad manner. Again, I surmised that any of us who happened to fly low over the Lines and do steep turns or a high-spirited roll was invariably rated as the Mad Major. Although there were supposed to be several competitors for the title, I never heard of anyone, especially a major, who expressly deserved it.

The infantrymen told me that there were Sherwood Foresters in the area, and I would have liked to contact them had I been able, for I might well have been with them had I not transferred to the R.F.C. Or, if not with them, under the sod with most of my platoon in the contingent of the 13th Battalion that went west in the Dardanelles, or with the brigade wiped out at Gommecourt on the Somme, or the others in the shambles at Thiepval.

While this informative little chat was going on, the rescue party from the squadron was held up at Dickebusch by the shelling. The sergeant-major had to find exactly where I was, not easy in the darkness and confusion, and he and his squad of men, who included my own fitter and rigger, had to walk up from the village and didn't arrive until after midnight. I was by then asleep in a dugout, but he woke me to say that he'd left the lorry and trailer in Dickebusch by the church, as the narrow lane to the lake was jammed with supply wagons.

As soon as they began to dismantle the Pup, the klaxons went, and we all had to put on respirators and seek cover. After half an hour we resumed work, but an hour later the gas alarms went again, and once more we had to stop. After another short spell of work, dawn broke, and the gunners said they must now camouflage the machine to hide it from Boche balloons.

I decided to stay on until next day, and sent the sergant-major and his party, less my own two men, to work under the camouflage, back to La Gorgue for sleep and food. Within a minute of their departure I was fast asleep in a dugout, and it seemed only seconds later when I was awakened by the shrill blast of a whistle. I scrambled to my feet and went outside, and yes, the battery sergeant-major had spotted another high-flying German reconnaissance plane, and we all froze until it went on.

This ritual amused me greatly, for as I pointed out to the major, it was impossible for an airman to distinguish human beings, still or moving, from even 10,000 feet, unless in mass, and, in any case, standing still didn't prevent battery positions being fixed by vertical photographs, or artillery observation planes or balloons. He shook his head dubiously, said maybe I was right, but orders were orders.

The day passed very like the day before, except that I tried to give a hand to the mechanics dismantling the plane, but soon realised that, working under the netting, I was more of a hindrance than a help. I left them and went with the major again to the O.P. to watch another shoot. Halfway through the morning, two Pups from the squadron came low over the battery, and flew round at fifty feet, the occupants waving. They were Courtneidge and Barrager, paying me a little call. The gunners were much elated by this shoot-up, which raised my stock considerably.

Once more there was a good deal of activity by our fighters and once more I watched a scrap taking place at about 8,000 feet some miles over. They were little more than specks, but I saw one drop out and dive down with smoke trickling behind it. Suddenly it burst into flames, became a ball of red fire, and plunged earthwards. The flames soon petered out, and the speck vanished, but the long trail of black smoke hung in the sky for quite a time.

In the afternoon the major urged me to get an anti-tetanus injection, as even a graze like mine could go wrong, so I set out in my fugboots, plus respirator and tin helmet, to find the Brigade Medical Officer, whose place was on the Ypres road beyond the northern end of the lake. But nobody knew where it was, and I was repeatedly misdirected until after two hours' tramping around I found myself on the outskirts of Ypres.

Once there, I thought, I might as well take a look at Wipers, as the troops called it, though there wasn't much to see, as few buildings had escaped serious damage from shelling. But it was interesting to walk among the ruins, the biggest pile being the famous Cloth Hall

I'd read about. There were numerous troops moving to and fro, and I later learned that thousands live in cellars and in the vaults under the citadel. There were some powerful smells about, too, from the decomposing corpses of horses lying off the roads.

Suddenly shells started falling, which smashed into the skeleton walls with so much dust and flying of bricks that I set off along the Dickebusch road. After a mile or so, I saw an R.A.M.C. dressing station in a half-destroyed cottage, which reminded me what I was there for, but I found only a corporal, who advised me to go to the artillery brigade's M.O. When I complained that I'd been looking for the place for half the afternoon, and was tired, he said, 'Why don't you take the train, sir?'

He wasn't joking. The line ran nearby, a narrow-gauge Deceauville with a light engine to take ammunition and other supplies to Ypres. I sat down by the track, lit a cigarette, and ten minutes later along came a miniature motor trolley driven by a large A.S.C. private. I finished the trip perched on one of his toy wagons. Eventually I found the dressing station and was duly jabbed.

As I walked into Dickebusch, darkness suddenly fell, and at once the road filled with traffic making for Ypres, guns, lorries, all kinds of other transport, even some rumbling tanks. All very interesting, but I had to get back to my machine. I stood at the roadside and asked several passing troops how to get to the lake, but they hadn't the foggiest notion, chum. Then the evening hate started, and I wandered on, with the traffic rattling on the cobbled road, wondering how I was to make contact with the squadron salvage party, due to arrive now.

At length, I saw a chink of light as a man came out of a house. I entered and saw that it was an Expeditionary Force canteen containing a score of troops drinking coffee. I ordered one and asked the man behind the counter how to reach the lake. He told me to turn off by the church opposite, and follow my nose till I fell in the water, chum.

There were two military policemen taking coffee, and I saw them staring hard at me, then they came up and asked who I was. I told them, but they were suspicious.

One said, 'We've been warned to look out for spies dressed as Flying Corps pilots. How did you get here?' I explained, and showed them my pocket-book, with letters addressed to me, but they weren't impressed.

'The Jerries can get that sort of thing from prisoners,' they said.

By this time everyone in the room was listening in, and also eyeing me in a nasty kind of way. I was getting riled, but managed to keep my temper.

'Look,' I said, 'there's a party from my squadron around here somewhere. Help me find them. They will identify me.' They dubiously agreed, and we crossed the road, with me in the centre, already practically under arrest, and turned the corner by the church. There by the cemetery wall was the lorry, waiting. The driver told me that the S.M. had gone forward with the trailer. The two M.P.s hastily apologised and disappeared in the darkness.

I set off for the lake, but the lane was filled with a slow-moving column of horse-drawn wagons, loaded with supplies. I sat on one, and learned from the driver that he belonged to 'my' battery, and thought that my luck was in at last, but then the gas alert went, the shells fell, and we all donned respirators. Some obstruction ahead caused a block, and there we were, stuck, with pockets of gas all round us. It wasn't pleasant to hear the horses and mules coughing and gasping as the fumes reached them. No gas-masks for them!

At length we got moving, and I was taken right to the doorstep. The S.M.'s party were loading the fuselage, wings and engine on to the trailer, which they'd managed to have towed up by an unengaged limber. While they were making everything tight, I bade my farewells to the major and his officers, and gathered my flying gear. We started back as soon as the lane was clear, but as we reached the village the Germans began shelling it again, and with some explosions uncomfortably close and shrapnel whirring in the darkness, none of us liked it overmuch.

On the slow journey home, along roads crammed with guns and supply columns and marching troops, I had plenty of time to reflect on my experiences of the past two days, and especially the constant diving for cover, the long hours wearing respirators, and never knowing whether the next shell hadn't your number on it. I decided that though we had our tricky moments in the R.F.C., our life was a picnic compared with the hellish existence that the P.B.I. and the gunners and the other forward fighting troops had to endure.

Never should I cease to thank my lucky stars for guiding me from the Sherwoods to the Flying Corps!

EIGHT
STILL ALIVE!

I woke at four o'clock, having been detailed the previous evening for the dawn patrol, but when I heard the beautiful music of rain pattering on the roof of my hut I dropped off to sleep again within seconds. During my brief time with the squadron I'd become so drilled to being called at set hours for the early patrols that I'd formed the habit of waking at four, six and eight o'clock, lying in a doze for a couple of minutes, then if neither an orderly nor my batman, Watt, appeared, and especially if there was the sound of rain, returning to slumber.

Watt finally called me just before eight with a cup of tea and the information that rain was pelting down and there was no flying. After breakfast and a trip to 'C' Flight hangar to check that my rigger was tightening up the controls of my Pup, I hadn't much to do, as it continued to pour heavily throughout the morning. I went into the Mess, crowded with the fellows playing vingt-un and poker, which didn't appeal to me, and leafed through the dog-eared newspapers and magazines, all of which I'd already seen. The readable books had been taken, and the only clean volume that looked a possible was *The Seven Lamps of Architecture*, but five minutes hard work on that made it clear why nobody had bothered to remove it. I too put it back on the shelf.

It was then that I decided that a browse through my flying log-book would be as interesting as anything, and it was, for when, sitting on the bed in my cubicle, I added up the flying times, I found that since my first flight with 46 Squadron I'd done fifty-four hours twenty-five minutes flying over the Lines. This surprised me, over fifty hours' war flying in five and a half weeks. And, even more surprising, I was still alive!

This was the first time I'd halted in my tracks to look back and reflect for a few minutes. How much had happened in those five weeks, to me as well as to my progression of flights and fights! As I listened gratefully to the rain, I let my mind dwell idly on the new horizons that had opened since I left England six weeks before, an immature youngster with only the slightest acquaintance with life and death.

From the moment when, after that unhappy trip across a rough Channel, I stepped for the first time upon the soil of France, I had run into a succession of entirely new experiences, some trivial, some stupendous. Even the early and unimportant ones remained as highlights in the memory: such as that first roisterous evening on *vin ordinaire* with my five pilot companions in our fusty, waterfront hotel at Boulogne: or the unexpected sight of some 2,000 chuckling Chinese labourers disembarking at the quayside from an impossibly small vessel: or the maddeningly dreary eight-hour journey in an undersized train to do the thirty-odd miles to St Omer: or the backstreet estaminet in which we were billeted, our meals taken at the long family table presided over by the stout, hairy patron in shirt-sleeves, the food served by his pretty daughter, the room delicately odoriferous from the urinal against the wall outside: or the long queues of British and Imperial troops waiting impatiently outside the licensed brothels: or the more refined officers' place, with a waiting room complete with out-of-date copies of *La Vie Parisienne*, right in the shadow of the Cathedral, which, as it was Sunday, was packed to the doors.

I recalled the days that followed in the Pilots' Pool at the Aircraft Depot south-west of the town, with little for us to do except lower each others' morale by exchanging rumours about the continuing heavy R.F.C. casualties in the Arras battles, or the inferiority of our aeroplanes, including the now obsolete Pup, compared with the German Albatros. Then, at last, the posting to 46 Squadron, the arrival of the Crossley tender, the cheerful friendly driver, the swift journey to yet another experience—an aerodrome only five miles from the front lines.

Although all these things had greatly widened my outlook, they did not count for much compared with what was to come. First was the event of becoming one of the compact circle of pilots in a fighter squadron. There was not the slightest gesture of welcome, yet the atmosphere of being a new boy, knowing nobody and disliked by everybody, had not lasted long, for each day I got to know a few of the pilots in my hut, or in my flight, and the ones I flew with on patrol. Then as more new boys arrived, I realised that there was a constant changing of the people about me as replacements came to make good casualties and those posted home at the end of their tour. Quite quickly, from being just faceless ciphers, we established personalities, became real people, members of the squadron.

We were a very mixed assembly, from every level, from all over Britain, all over the Empire. Some had come almost straight from school to the R.F.C., others from infantry regiments, the artillery, cavalry, engineers. Some, like me, had come because they were eager to fly, others for the eight shillings a day flying pay, which I, as a married man, found more than useful to supplement my second lieutenant's seven-and-sixpence. Still others came for no other reason than to escape the purgatory of the trenches.

We lived to a rhythmic pattern, mounting into the air two or three times a day to do battle, then returning to our pleasant Mess, to enjoy an exclusive, comfortable existence, like cattle being fattened for the slaughterhouse. But we didn't see it that way. We had our daily job to do, and it was strange how, overnight, we became accustomed to the routine—of having a good breakfast after a good night's sleep, then going up on the mid-morning patrol, taking part in a frantic dog-fight three miles high, killing a young German, who'd also had a good night's sleep and a good breakfast in a comfortable Mess, then probably narrowly escaping being killed oneself before coming down, having a swim, a drink, a good lunch. All quite the normal, one hardly commented on it after a while—like going to the office.

Isolated from the rest of the world, we didn't really care, for we were not interested in it. Certainly we read the newspapers, a day or two late, with eagerness, for otherwise we would not have known how our war was progressing, but we soon forgot even the boldest headlines, and took such momentous events as the Russian Revolution and the death of Kitchener in our stride as being of lesser consequence than reports that Baron Richtofen was shooting down too many British airmen.

Our strongest links with the outer world were the letters to and from home, but those we wrote were usually brief and perfunctory. We had little contact even with other R.F.C. squadrons, though some were within easy flying distance. Religion did not intrude, except at funerals. Occasionally we went to La Gorgue village for a cinematograph show or an army concert or a hot bath in the brewery. Or we took advantage of transport going to Merville, St Omer or Doullens, where we had a meal or did needless shopping, while the more enterprising patronised a brothel.

With the other ranks we had little to do, except the particular N.C.O.s and mechanics who serviced our planes and guns, and without whose unglamorised devotion we couldn't have flown at all. But the R.F.C. was different from the rest of the army, where officers and men shared both hardship and the hazards of combat, whereas with us, only pilots and observers and air gunners did the fighting. There was a barrier, unspoken but real, of which the men were more conscious than we were, but which served to throw us pilots closer together in our tight little community.

Yet this fraternity, in spite of its common perils and pleasures, was no infallible sphere for strong, enduring friendships. It was not only that we were never a band of entirely amicable brethren, for there were always some who heartily disliked others, and for no discernible reason, though in the air, all such differences vanished. It was that too often there was insufficient time to get to know a man before he disappeared over the other side. Our casualties were probably no higher than those of other fighter squadrons, yet since my arrival we had lost three killed and three missing, one of whom we later learned was killed, and two wounded. All three missing pilots were with us only a matter of days, and it was during the dangerous initial period that fighter pilots most frequently met their fate.

I was one of the fortunate group who managed to keep alive long enough to make several friends, and I had survived largely because of good advice received on almost my first day, and from another newcomer at that. 'For your first fortnight,' he said sagely, 'don't think of trying to shoot down Huns, just concentrate on not being shot down yourself.' He'd learned that from a flying instructor in England who'd done a tour as a scout pilot in France.

The reason my own flight commander did not tell me this, nor any of the senior pilots in the squadron, was because they did not know, for they'd had no fighter experience. Until a week or so before I came, they'd been flying two-seater reconnaissance Nieuports, and so they, and we, had to learn our air fighting the hard way.

And now, over five weeks later, I had established a few notions about how to survive. First, you just had to have good luck. Second, you had to know when to run away while you had the chance. Third, a Pup wasn't the machine for rash aggression. Fourth, you could become a Hun-getter by guts, luck, straight shooting and having a lethal aeroplane. In 46 Squadron, we did not have a really lethal aeroplane, for though the Pup had been an effective fighter a year or more before, it had long since been left behind by the Albatros D–III. And we knew it, which was no stiffener to morale.

What saved us from being shot down in droves like B.E.s and R.E.s and F.E.8s and D.H.2s and Sopwith and Nieuport two-seaters was the Pup's agility at all heights, which made us a difficult target in a dog-fight, and which even gave us a chance to twist in behind an inexperienced Hun and shoot him down. But once engaged in a fight we couldn't withdraw, for the Pup was slower than every German fighter by a good margin.

After my five weeks' war flying, I still hadn't shot down a single

Above: Top scorers of 46 Squadron. *Left:* G.E. Thompson, 21 victories. *Right:* D.R MacLaren, 54 victories, sixth in list of British aces (with R. Gilmour) *Below:* Baron Manfred von Richtofen on convalescent leave, with head wound

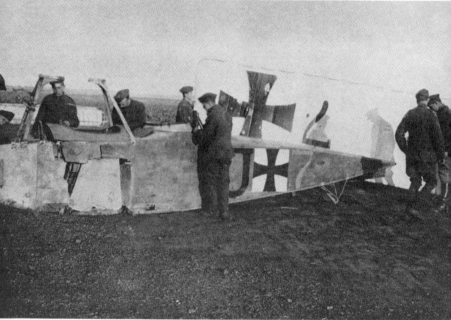

Above: Albatros C-I two-seater
Below: R.F.C mechanics dismantling Albatros C-V/16 two-seater

Hun, but I didn't complain, I was satisfied with avoiding being shot down myself, and I was learning. From what I heard afterwards, some of our top fighter pilots[1] took a time to learn the trick of becoming an ace. If I eventually flew a killer plane, such as a Camel or an S.E., I might with continuing luck shoot down my proper ration of the enemy. But there was no hope of glory for a Pup pilot on the Ypres front in the spring and summer of 1917, for opposed to us were some of the most skilled and experienced scout pilots in the German Air Force, of whom Voss, Allmenröder and Manfred and Lothar Richtofen were but typical.

With an odd feeling that I was looking back over months rather than weeks, I glanced at the entries in my log-book from the day of my arrival. Almost every one held some special significance in the memory. My first flight from La Gorgue aerodrome, for example, when I saw the Lines from 10,000 feet, that unbelievable shell-pitted belt of trenches and barbed wire, where the corpses of hundreds of thousands of men, British and German, had rotted away into the soil, was certainly one of my most impressive experiences.

Everything below was so very full of interest that I set about checking the map to locate not only cities of which I'd read and heard so much, such as Ypres and Armentières and Lille, but less easily identified places such as Loos, La Bassée, Ploegsteert Wood, Polygon Wood and other scenes of fierce fighting. Then and on my first patrols, my gaze was too much drawn to this history on the ground, and I was inclined to forget that my job was really to look out for Huns. But I soon passed through this phase, for I learned that if I wished to go on living, I had to discover the presence of Huns before they could draw near enough to hit me.

And how difficult this was at the beginning, when I couldn't spot an enemy machine until it was within stone-throwing distance. Or

[1] McCudden, for example, destroyed only two Huns in his first three months, while Beauchamp-Proctor spent his first five months, and on S.E.5a's at that, without a single Hun, yet ended the war as our fifth top-scorer, with fifty-four victories. Similarly, McElroy, with forty-nine victories, gained none during his first five months.

even worse, as on my very first patrol, in my very first skirmish, when I never saw the Huns at all! Suddenly the formation leader had briefly rocked his wings and disappeared. One moment he was there, fixed in space ahead, and the next he'd gone. Out of the corner of my eye, I realised that the third member of our formation wasn't there either. I dived after them in a panic, my inexperienced eye unable to find them until I saw below me the tracer from their guns firing at something. But at what? On full throttle I caught them up, wildly excited, thumb on trigger, eye glued to the Aldis sight—but nothing to fire at. Only later did I learn that we had attacked three Albatros scouts, but that they had quickly turned away eastwards.

Such was my inglorious initiation into air fighting. Then, as the log-book entry showed two days later, came the evening patrol during which I fired my first shots in anger, not at a dog-fight opponent but at a high-flying two-seater whose observer had the audacity to attack me from below when I was alone, at 18,000 feet, gazing at the dying sun's red glow over distant England. This was the first time I'd been close enough to a German aeroplane to see the occupants, the first time I realised that I was fighting men, not machines. It was the first time too that I looked into the flash of machine-guns firing at *me* at a hundred yards' range, watched the tracer coming apparently into my face, and my tracer doing the same to the observer. Then the pilot dived away and so nothing came of that encounter. But again I'd learned something—never to be off the alert, even in the late evening, even with a ravishingly glorious sunset to distract me.

Another entry a few days on recorded the occasion when my leader, Joske, attacked a two-seater, and we found we'd fallen into an ambush. Joske pulled clear in time, but I didn't, and escaped destruction only by diving vertically with full engine from 12,000 feet to 500, with six Albatroses firing at me down to 1,000. This used up too much of my luck, six to one, each with two Spandau guns, and I wasn't even wounded, though the poor old Pup was badly savaged. I still don't know why my wings didn't fold back. Joske reported me as shot down, and I'd already been reported missing previously, yet I was still around. But this did mean that I had to be careful to touch wood before a scrap, an early detail of my education, and quite simple, as there was plenty of wood within reach in the cockpit.

It was after this particular episode that I was first assailed by secret fears. In the daytime, I was seldom conscious of real fear, except in brief, gasping moments of combat, but sometimes, lying awake in the night, thinking over the hair's breadth escapes of the day, I would ask myself, Have I the guts to see the job through? For a time I wasn't sure, for I suspected that I wasn't born to be a hero, but gradually as I saw that luck was always with me, the secret fears died away—at any rate for a time.

One line in the log-book was starred to mark an encounter, not with enemy aircraft, but with accurate archie. On my earlier patrols, the black woolly balls of smoke had always burst at a safe distance, for our formation leaders knew the trick of slight deviations of course which deceived the archie gunners below. But on this occasion, as the three of us were diving after a D.F.W. two-seater, archie came to his aid with four good sighting shots about fifty yards ahead. I heard their loud coughs, then as we flew through the pungent smoke, the second and third salvos exploded around us, and one burst directly under me with an earsplitting roar.

The startled Pup shot up fifty feet with a jerk that sent the blood to my ankles. I waited in cringing tension for the plane to fold up, then as I found I was all in one piece, started breathing again, a long deep breath of relief. I handled the Pup with excessive gentleness for the rest of the patrol, and on landing found that she had been gashed in a dozen places, yet no serious injury had been done.

When archie got as close as this, the bursts didn't come with the doggy *wuff! wuff!* of a distant shot, nor even the deep *crump! crump!* of one fifty yards away, but with a tearing, deafening *crash!* that stopped everything in your body, and made you feel, God I *am* dead this time! Excessively bad for the heart. But on this occasion nothing else developed and we flew on seemingly undamaged. Almost I was sorry for the archie gunners, to see no result for their dead-on-the-target shooting. But although we escaped unhurt, as we'd done often enough before, accurate archie was one of the unpleasantries of the air war to which I knew I'd never become accustomed.

My eye ran down the two pages of entries for June. The dog-fight when I first experienced the thrill of real in-fighting, a confused, breathless circling to avoid being tailed, those few spasmodic bursts at targets too fleeting to hit, steep-banking Albatros D–IIIs, all gaily coloured, in sharp contrast with our uniform drab brown. The whole hectic action over within three minutes, and quite indecisive, the Huns didn't like fighting us at 17,000. But at least I had some notion of what was going on, and I knew better what to do next time—and that was the important thing, there would be a next time, I hadn't been shot down.

A further entry, the same day, recalled the first flamer I'd seen fall down the sky, the red burning plane with the trail of black smoke above, while I gazed fascinated, scarcely able to stomach the realisation of what was happening to a fellow flyer, British or German. This too was something I could never accustom myself to watch without an uneasy shiver.

Four lines down, and a patrol that was eventless except for yet another new experience. Towards its end, while we were making southwest, still on the Hun side of the Lines, a blaze of red appeared suddenly on my right. Momentarily, I thought that the pilot in echelon behind me had fired a Very cartridge to my flank, but then I realised what it was, one of our balloons falling in flames about three miles away. The sky around it was pinpointed with the bursting shells of our archie, but half a minute later a second balloon fell. They went down slowly at first, blazing masses of red and yellow, then collapsed and dropped quickly, leaving a vast pall of red-tinted smoke suspended above. We dived steeply to try to catch the Hun fighters who had done the job, but were far too late, and never saw them.

Yet another memorable entry, another first experience that I didn't enjoy at all, was when my engine cut out at 17,000 feet when the patrol was miles over the Lines. The others swept on, for there was nothing they could do, and I swung west. To have to glide back alone, crippled and defenceless, at the mercy of any Hun that might come along, was even more unnerving than accurate archie, especially with the harrowing possibility that I could never reach our side of the Lines. I only just made it, and had a hair-raising minute as the target for hundreds of rifles and machine-guns as I glided across the trenches at well under 500 feet.

To be shot down in combat was a risk one faced with a shrug of the shoulders, but to be forced down through engine failure was a possibility one took ill, yet even the unflagging service given by our fitters could not rule out the chance of some purely mechanical breakdown. It was just a matter of good fortune. Had my engine failed a mile further east, I would have been a prisoner.

Looking back over the happenings of the past six weeks, I saw that I was still alive because of three things. The first was the sheer good luck with which I'd been favoured time and time again. Second, unlike most newcomers to fighter squadrons, with their fifteen hours and less flying experience, I'd done over eighty, and was by comparison a skilled pilot, with at least a chance of holding my own against seasoned Huns. And third, the Pup almost made up for what she lacked in speed and armament by her light control, her easy manœuvre and her unexpected sturdiness.

Even during my first flights on Pups during training days, I realised what a likeable plane she was, so gentle and responsive yet so spirited, so eager to co-operate, as though she were a living thing. In England, I was always told to handle her with care, for her structure was fragile, she could easily break up under stress, but now I knew differently. After my vertical 12,000-foot dive with racing engine, I knew that though she did not enjoy such discourtesies, she would stand anything bar sheer ham-fisted clumsiness.

So docile a creature was meant to be flown for fun, not for killing, and in France she was never a Hun-getter like the Camel I was to fly later. Long afterwards I was to discover that not one of the top British aces piled up his list of victories on Pups. Even the Nieuport, especially in the hands of such pilots as Ball and Bishop, was more efficiently lethal, though never on the same level as the Camel and the S.E.5a.

Yet despite her deficiencies for aggressive fighting, the Pup, at all heights, could be as evasive as a butterfly, and this quality had saved me from extinction on half-a-dozen occasions. Small wonder that as I skimmed through the record of dangers shared with her, I could feel sentimental about her, could hold even an affection for both the machines I flew and for the breed, for they were thoroughbreds.

And as the rain spattered still on the roof, I thanked my lucky stars for the day, months before, when instead of being sent to France to fly the death-traps on which others like me were condemned to sacrifice their liberty or their lives, I was chosen to be trained on 'Scouts'—and so began my rewarding love affair with the matchless Pup.

NINE

DISTANT OFFENSIVE PATROL

Halfway through a hot and humid July morning I was one of five Pup pilots flying eastwards at 12,000 feet on a Distant Offensive Patrol. We had just passed across the Lines, and behind us hung a forlorn procession of slowly dissolving shapes of black smoke, the wraiths of archie bursts. The sky was massed with untidy banks of ragged cloud reaching up a couple of thousand feet or more above us, while much higher, at over 20,000 feet, spread scattered sheets of feathery cirrus.

We were flying in a loose vic formation, and I was at the rear of its right arm, a subordinate position because we were drawn from both 'B' and 'C' Flights, and the two from 'B' were senior to me. Not that this worried me, but there were other things that did. I faced this patrol with no great ardour, first because, like every other fighter pilot, I did not relish D.O.P.s, and, second, because I did not trust my engine. Not only was it running roughly but it lacked power, and even at full throttle I had, during the past few thousand feet, as we entered into rarer air, fought a losing battle to keep station.

As, hastened by a twenty-five miles an hour wind, we quickly penetrated German-held territory, I realised that the four planes suspended in space beside me were gradually drawing away. Hanging on my prop, I steadily lost position until at 15,000 feet, I was over a hundred yards behind. And there was little I could do except wait for the leader of the formation, Captain Scott, to look round. Had the engine positively failed, I could have dived in front, given the distress signal and gone home, but I couldn't do that merely because the Le Rhône was off colour. Nor was my condition desperate enough to justify firing a green distress signal. And so I limped along like a lame duck until I had fallen 200 yards back, an easy and immediate victim for any Hun patrol that might roar up from the rear.

What made my predicament the worse was that as one of the two rearward pilots I shared the main responsibility for keeping watch for astern attacks. At last, just when I felt that there was no alternative to firing the Very light, Scott turned his head, saw me in trouble and throttled back until I caught up, after which he continued at a more sedate rate of climb.

We were then about five miles into Hunland, and as I reflected that we had still ten miles or more to go, I realised that I was glad we were being led by Scott, for he knew what he was doing. He had been with 46 Squadron as 'C' Flight commander for only a few weeks, but he'd come from 54 Squadron, which had served in France with Pups for over six months compared with 46's six weeks, and whose every experienced pilot knew how Pups should be handled tactically, while even our flight-commanders were only just learning.

Scott had already shown himself to be very pugnacious in the air, but he had also shown that he knew when to act with caution. When he took over 'C' Flight he told us that he meant to see that his flight shot down its share of Huns, but not, if he could help it, at the sacrifice of any of his pilots. He said our first job as scout pilots was to stay alive, and that applied especially to newcomers, for every fight we survived gave us a little more experience and a better chance to get through the next one.

We knew that he shared our lack of enthusiasm for D.O.P.s, and also that he was more than alert to the tactical limitations of the Pup, for he had explained before we set off that he would seek no dogfights when miles over the Lines except on his own terms, which meant at 17,000 feet and above, where we could out fly the Albatros.

At lower altitudes, all five of us could well be written off, as had happened to less cautiously led patrols of Pups in the recent past.

When we met an enemy formation he had said, we must entice it up to our level before attacking, and if it refused to be enticed, we'd have to be content with dive and zoom. If so, he hoped we'd shoot straight, as there would probably be opportunity for only one or two bursts each dive, and if we let ourselves be drawn into a lower-level scrap, there'd be little chance of getting clear, especially with a strong westerly wind against us as usual.

This all made sense to us, and we followed him in full confidence that he'd take no harebrained chances, despite the fact that we were going to trail our coats, looking for trouble. And as we swept on eastwards, I saw that the weather was changing, the masses of cloud were becoming more solid-looking and rising now almost to our height of 16,000 feet. And of course the temperature was falling rapidly, and I began to shiver with the penetrating cold. Scott fired a few shots every so often to keep his gun warm, and we did the same.

Occasionally my gaze dropped briefly to the earth below, very distant now, and because we were well clear of the Lines and their ramifications, everything looked normal, neat and map-like, and in areas where there were rivers and woodlands, enticingly inviting. Yet to us it was all hostile country, and we would become prisoners should we descend there. But one's eyes did not rest long on the ground, for the main preoccupation now was looking for Huns. And this was not a matter of an occasional glance round, but of methodically examining the skies and the clouds, above, below, behind and ahead, to discover in good time those remote specks which could so quickly materialise into bellicose Hun scouts with flashing Spandau guns.

Certainly we had to look downwards too, where planes could be more difficult to pick up against the mosaic of fields and woods than against sky and cloud. To facilitate this search we constantly but very slightly swung and tilted our machines to uncover the blind arcs directly behind and underneath, and above the upper wings. In addition, we frequently looked up towards the sun, masking its glare with a thumb close to the eye, for there was always the chance that a Hun patrol might be higher than us.

The trouble with this ceaseless searching of the skies behind was that you needed a rubber neck, especially when you were at the rear of the formation, and even more especially when flying fifteen miles inside Hunland, when attack could come from any quarter. Because you were tightly belted to your seat, you could only slightly twist your body, and during a two-hour distant patrol, the incessant neck twisting was not only fatiguing but a cause of aches and pains for hours afterwards.

Certainly you had the mirror attached to the right centre-section strut, but it covered only a small disc of the panorama behind, and should you ever spot a Hun in it, you could say your prayers, because he'd be within easy shooting distance.

The ability to spot and identify enemy planes at a distance came chiefly by experience, and that was where the older members of the squadron, or like Scott of other squadrons, were at a great advantage. After several weeks' practice, I could pick up the distant specks early enough, but I hadn't developed Scott's hawk-like eye, which could identify the specks as Huns, almost by instinct, before I could even make out the shape, and long before I could definitely recognise the type.

By now we were over Courtrai, some fifteen miles into what our Canadian pilots called the back country, and Scott turned there, and began our beat to the south, twenty miles down to Tournai, then swung back again to Courtrai, then south again and so on until our time was up or until the Germans assembled a much stronger formation and sent it aloft to overwhelm us. After all, they had ample time to do this. No doubt they thought we were completely insane, and may be the high-ups who ordered such patrols were.

I noted that to avoid being blown further east by our unrelenting enemy, the prevailing westerly wind, we were crabbing south-south-west. This prevailing wind was a constant influence on our tactics, and also on our morale, for not only could it hinder or even prevent a crippled pilot or machine from reaching the British Lines, but in a prolonged dog-fight, every minute saw the formation being carried further and further into enemy territory.

We reached Tournai without incident, turned, crabbed north-north-west back to Courtrai, then turned south again. Just as I was thinking that it was about time for Scott to consider the idea of going home, I noticed him staring intently to the east. I too searched the eastern skies, my gaze slowly moving across the whole vast area, but I could see nothing. Yet Scott still peered in the same direction, and I looked again. This time I saw, well below us, a group of tiny specks, like a bunch of dancing midges, six or seven maybe, just visible against a wall of grey cloud. Even as I discovered them, they waltzed round its edge and disappeared. So our coat-trailing had worked. Huns were on the way up without a doubt, but too far away and too low for action, though of course we'd wait for them to come up.

Meanwhile Scott continued on our southward track, and the five of us were alone in the sky, five machines seemingly a single organism suspended in space. Apart from the slight dips and lifts to keep formation and gentle imbalances to augment search, there was no feeling that we were moving at over ninety miles an hour, whether in relation to each other, or to the cloud banks below; or to the more remote earth. The only movement within the organism came from the fluttering pennants of the leader and deputy, the constantly turning helmeted heads of the pilots, and the gently oscillating ailerons and elevators as they responded to minute adjustments of the joystick. And of course the revolving propellers that kept us aloft, they did move, but so swiftly that nothing could be seen save a transparent disc that sometimes caught and flashed the rays of the sun.

Our celestial little world was without noise too, for the roar of an engine was the normal, noticed only when it faltered or stopped in shattering silence. The only sounds that might impinge on our seclusion would be the crackle of bullets or the crash of bursting archie shells. Even my engine, though still running unevenly compared with the usual smooth purr of the Le Rhône, did not vary in its note, and so long as this song continued unchanged, I might not have to worry unduly.

Suddenly I realised that Scott was changing course, swinging towards a mountain of cumulus that had lifted up on our left flank, for the cloud masses were changing their formations and heights as they scudded eastwards under the high wind. We reached the cloud, and followed its bulging curves all the way round it until we were facing west. I knew that Scott was stalking Huns, but search as I might, I couldn't find them.

The cloud was left behind us as we passed in the clear towards another, rising at us from the west. Then I saw them, a group of planes climbing hard beyond the further side of the new cloud. We were at 17,000, and they were over two thousand feet below, and it seemed as though Scott was leading us up behind them, hoping to effect a surprise attack from the east.

The enemy formation could have been the same half-dozen that I'd seen previously, but much nearer than they were before. I could still not positively identify them, though from the distinctive way they sat on their tails in their steep climb, they were Albatroses. As I looked, I noted that one of them was lagging behind and below the others. A failing engine and an anxious pilot. How well I knew that feeling! As I watched, he gave up the tussle, dipped down from the formation and within a few seconds had disappeared below. For him merely an inconvenience, provided he was a fair pilot and didn't crash, for he would land among friends and be back in his Mess for lunch, no doubt.

But a very different fate would have awaited one of us. On my last D.O.P., in which five Pups had carried out a sweep with five Nieuport Scouts, stepped a thousand feet below us, I saw, when we were twelve miles over, one of the Nieuports leave his formation and go down, just as the Hun had done. But for him there was the bitter sight of the others speeding on, then the slow glide to earth, naked under the guns of any passing Hun, then the forced landing, the welcoming party of German troops, with no chance even to set the machine alight. Then the tame surrender, the bullying, the interrogations, the probable ill-treatment, and the despatch to a prison camp, there to rot away for years. What a hell to have to face, not as a result of a fight in which one had been worsted, and from which one was glad to have emerged alive, but because some damned screw or spring or petrol pipe had broken.

The sweep with the Nieuports had been eventless so far as fighting was concerned, for no Huns were seen, much less encountered, yet a pilot and aeroplane had been lost, and with no gain whatever. This was the kind of risk that nagged us throughout our D.O.P.s, not the risk of being downed in a fight. We accepted the hazards of combat, but we did not willingly accept the hazard of losing our freedom, and maybe our lives, simply because we had to go too far east to get home if the engine failed or was hit by a bullet or if one was wounded.

The futility of such wasteful losses was the deeper because if a D.O.P. were weak in numbers, as we were now, it could easily be overwhelmed, but if the patrol were strong, the Germans could, and frequently did, ignore it, leaving us with a debit of forced-landed aeroplanes, wasted engine hours and wasted petrol.

Had there been a specific object in our deep penetrations, such as covering a bombing raid or a photographic reconnaissance, we would have thought nothing of it, but we could see no rational purpose in our coat-trailing D.O.P.s. We could not see what was achieved by this so-called carrying of the offensive into enemy territory. Was it to impress the French or discourage German troops? But they could hardly see us at 15,000 feet up. Was it to lower the morale of the German Air Forces? This notion we found laughable, for ours was the morale that suffered.

Then did we find more fights or shoot down more Huns by going fifteen miles into their territory? On the contrary, combats were fewer, for the really intensive fighting was always near the Lines, within reach of the artillery-spotting and other patrolling two-seaters.

Unfortunately High Command held to the illusion that D.O.P.s not only produced bigger and better combats but were an important instrument of offensive policy, which was a meaningless slogan, for an offensive spirit in the air meant attacking the enemy with resolution, not showing the flag over Tournai. The consequence was that fighter pilots built up a deep resentment against being exposed to unnecessary risks on D.O.P.s which sense and experience showed were usually pointless.

These insubordinate notions did not all come unbidden in the air but later on the ground, when there was time and mood to reflect. And now I was jerked out of my doleful thoughts about the lost Nieuport by Scott suddenly rocking his wings. He had told us, when ordering dive and zoom attacks against Huns well below us, not only to shoot straight but to fire short bursts, for if we failed to conserve ammunition and a prolonged combat developed, we should be left without the wherewithal to fight. As we hadn't the speed to run away, there'd be nothing else to do but spin down to imprisonment as the alternative to being slaughtered.

Scott began a shallow dive, with three-quarters throttle. I could see the six enemy V-strutters beneath and to our front, and it looked as though we might surprise them. Flying in a loose group, they were still climbing, and going directly away from us to the north-west, clearly silhouetted against a cloud beyond. But surely they were watching their tails, surely they had seen us, I thought, and then I re-alised—we were diving on them out of the sun. Crafty Scott! This was why he'd manoeuvred so patiently.

Then the thought suddenly struck me. What about *our* tails? I turned my head to look right behind, and my heart nearly stopped. There, directly astern, coming round the cloud we'd just left, was an-other group of V-strutters, roaring after us with smoking exhausts. This was no time for shilly-shallying! Still in the dive, growing steeper now, I lifted up the Very pistol, held the joystick between my knees, drew a red cartridge and placed it in the pistol, then fired it forward and above. The flare soared alongside the formation and plunged down away to the right.

Alerted, Scott slackened the dive, turned, saw me rocking my wings frantically and pointing rearwards. Then he spotted the pursu-ing Huns, immediately switch-backed the dive into a climb, and swung us due west. By the look of it we had fallen into a trap, for the Germans had sent up two Jastas after us, and while we were stalk-ing one, the other was stalking us. Unfortunately we had lost a thousand feet of our precious height in our dive, and Scott was trying to regain it before facing up to our more urgent danger, the pack yelping behind, six of them as far as I could make out. But they were climbing too. I glanced down at the other formation and saw that they had swung north and were also climbing hard.

I did not like the situation at all. If Scott engaged the group behind, they would tie us down until the second group reached our level, and then there would be twelve D–IIIs against five Pups. I began to feel scared, for we wouldn't have a hope. But Scott would surely have kept an eye on the lower formation. As I looked towards him he showed that he had seen, and that he did not intend to be trapped so easily. Still climbing, he turned towards a vast pile of cumulus on our left, waved his arms to signify 'open out', and led us into its towering flank.

I always disliked being engulfed in the dark dampness of heavy cloud, especially when other planes were near me, and I took the precaution of easing the rudder gently, so as to edge a few degrees to starboard. It was a nervy feeling, five of us flying blind, and anyone might veer from his course or level, and then a glancing collision. And no parachutes!

But within a minute, light glowed ahead and we issued into sunlight. We had opened the formation considerably, and were at different levels, but we were still five. Before I could look round for the Huns, Scott swung right, slowed down while we re-formed on him, then continued the climb alongside the cloud. I began to drop behind again, for he was on full throttle. Looking back over my tail, I saw that the pursuing Huns had not followed us through the cloud, but had gone round it, and were now below us and further away. As they resumed the chase, I saw the second formation coming up steeply, now only a thousand feet under us. What on earth could Scott do to get us out of this mess?

Suddenly he banked us round forty-five degrees in a sharp turn, rocked his wings violently, and dipped at once into a dive towards the lower formation. What the hell, I thought, this is wrong, the others will drop on us now. As we swooped steeply down, I moved out

115

to the right, clear of the machine in front. The D–IIIs rushed up towards us. I saw the black crosses, the variegated colourings, picked out a black and silver in checks, a fine-looking beast, and centred him in the Aldis. A second later they awoke to their danger, and began to scatter as Scott's tracer sped away at 300 yards, and ours followed a split second later.

I fired in steady bursts of about twenty rounds. On the third burst, the checkered plane, whose swerve I had followed, reared up high, fell over on its side, then dropped below. Maybe I'd hit him, maybe he was just pulling out of a tight corner. There was no time to switch to another target, as we were now too close, and I was waiting tensely for Scott to zoom. But he didn't zoom. He took us right through the middle of the swirling group. How we avoided collisions I don't know. They broke wildly in vertical banks, and I all but cut into the elevator of one of them with my port wing. I was running with sweat, for a narrow escape from collision always frightened me.

What the hell are you up to, Scott? I cried indignantly, now we'll have the whole crowd on us. We were still diving steeply, but Scott began to level out in a smooth curve while turning towards the west. I gave a hasty glance back, and there they were, two distinct formations, converging on us in a steep dive. There were only ten all told, so we had sent a couple down in our dive attack. I then looked forward again, and once more my heart nearly stopped. Two more formations were coming towards us from the west, one of them on our level, the other 500 feet higher. My poor heart now sank right to the bottom of my flying boots. Not *more* Huns!

Then I saw—and shouted with relief, for now I understood Scott's apparent rashness. There were two flights of Camels, six apiece, which he had spotted in the distance when he suddenly turned and dived. And now the Huns spotted them too. As we came round in a tight curve behind and above the Camels, so that we faced the oncoming enemy, I felt I could see them hesitate, I could follow the workings of their minds. This is an ambush, they decided, twelve Camels and five Pups and we're only ten, we haven't a chance.

But they continued the dive, began firing, and the tracers stabbed down, not at us but at the Camels, which at once began to open out for a dog-fight. But the Huns swung off to the flanks in two untidy groups and dived steeply away to the east. The Camels immediately dived after them, and the whole crowd, enemy and friend, disappeared within seconds.

Scott gave no sign of any intention to follow, but instead started off at once to the westwards. I glanced at the dashboard watch and knew what he was thinking. Our petrol duration was three hours at the most, we'd been over Hunland for over two hours, we'd previously taken half an hour to reach patrol height, and we now had to get back to the Lines against a twenty-five mile an hour headwind. I checked our position, saw the smoky mass of Turcoing and Roubaix ahead, and realised that we had over fifteen miles to go.

The journey back was not amusing, for there was every chance of running into an enemy patrol and being forced into a dog-fight, which might end with us all going down with empty tanks. Fortunately we met no Huns, but just as I relaxed at the thought that we were all set except for archie, my engine began to miss. The revs dropped, and with them my speed, and within minutes I was lagging well behind.

This time the wideawake Scott saw my predicament, and stalled the four down to my speed to escort me across the Lines. By then I was losing height, and because of our slow progress, archie gave us a most unpleasant buffeting, which even Scott's sly evasions couldn't much mitigate. We were all hit, some several times, including me. My nastiest bull's-eye gave me a shock. Shells were bursting well below us when there was suddenly a tremendous clang! under my seat. I felt the impact on my posterior and waited like a coiled up spring for some part of my machine to fall away, but nothing did.

When I reached home, my rigger found that a jagged piece of shell-casing some three inches long had penetrated the metal seat, but because it was almost spent, had been held by the padded cushion. I thanked my lucky stars to have escaped a very inconvenient wound.

As soon as we were over the trenches, Scott gave the washout, and

I was left by myself. The Le Rhône was still missing intermittently, but it managed to keep me in flight on the glide, and had taken me nearly halfway to La Gorgue when suddenly it petered out. I knew from the splutter that I'd exhausted my petrol after all, but luckily for me well on my side of the trenches. I made a passable forced landing in a field south-west of Ploegsteert Wood, next to an army camp, from which I telephoned the squadron. I was late for lunch, but probably no more so than the Hun who went down this morning.

Scott greeted me with 'Good show, Lee, spotting those bastards on our tails. But get yourself another engine—lame ducks sometimes have to be left behind.'

TEN
COMBAT REPORT

I was the second to touch down, and as I taxied to the hangars I saw Odell follow me and make a neat landing. Two other Pups were circling above prior to coming in. Outside 'C' Flight hangar I pulled up alongside Scott's machine, unloaded my Vickers, made sure the armourer retrieved the ejected rounds, then inspected the splintered fairing at the right-hand side of the cockpit. A close group of three or four bullets had gone neatly through, having passed close over my right shoulder. Another bullet had scraped along the side of the Vickers, leaving a streak of lead, but so far as I could see, it had done no damage.

While I clambered down, my rigger gave the machine a quick look-over.

'A bunch of nine bullets through your starboard lower wing, sir,' he announced, 'and four on each side of the fuselage. One lot in at an angle, the other going out. But until I open the fabric I can't say whether there's any damage.'

I pointed to the splintered fairing, and told him to make a thorough check forward. Then I called the armourer, and asked him to inspect the gun, and preferably try it out on the butts. I flung off my leather coat and helmet and gloves, and dumped them on a wing, then went to Scott's machine. There I found why he'd had to fire a green Very light and return. His interrupter gear had gone wrong while he was firing, and he'd shot away half his propeller. Hence the glide home from 18,000 feet from nearly five miles over, with the rest of the patrol acting as escort.

Meanwhile the two others had landed and taxied in. Only five all told so far. The missing pilot was Ferrie, a Canadian, the most recent arrival in the squadron, who had already shown his mettle in previous patrols. He'd certainly not been shot down, we'd seen him at the end of the fighting. Maybe he'd had a forced landing. We forgot him for the moment while we gathered in an animated group around Scott's machine.

We'd had a stirring fight towards the end of the patrol, and everyone was talking loudly and rapidly about what had happened. Some were almost incoherent, others gesticulating wildly, everyone laughing easily. We were in that excited, voluble condition that always followed a patrol with a scrap in it, as though we'd actually enjoyed the thrill of danger.

'Where's Ferrie?' suddenly asked Scott. 'Not back yet? Anybody see him drop out?'

Nobody had noticed when he'd left us when we streamed home in a loose formation after Scott's washout.

'Any distress signal?' continued Scott. 'Well, a dud engine perhaps. Or maybe he was hit. . . .'

We gaze eastwards. No plane in sight. Then again putting him out of our minds we turned to each others' accounts of the encounter of twenty minutes ago.

We'd gone out on the second morning patrol, five of us from 'C' Flight, including the leader, Captain Scott, and one, Ferrie, from 'B'. The sky was a pale blue, with banks of cumulus building up to 10,000 feet. After over an hour and a half of fruitless beating north and south among the white tops of the clouds, some five miles in German-held territory, without seeing any enemy planes, Scott turned further eastwards, climbing steadily.

It was when we'd reached 17,000, and were turning in a wide half-circle to come westwards, that a formation of eight Albatros D–IIIs appeared from the east, about 1,000 feet above. They had the ad-

vantage of the sun, and were able to come uncomfortably close before Scott spotted them. A few seconds after he rocked his wings in
warning, they dived, but we were already swerving, and although
their tracers seemed to be everywhere they hit nobody. They zoomed
up from the initial dive and came down again, but this time we swung
up at them as they swirled above us, and a dog-fight started.

At 17,000 feet the lightly loaded Pup was able to hold its own,
and more, against the Albatros, with its massive Mercedes engine and
heavy turn. A fierce, confusing mêlée followed in which it was difficult for anybody to keep his sights on any target for more than two
or three seconds. The Albatroses, though they scored hits in snap
bursts, could not nail down their nimble opponents for the kill, and,
as for us, whenever we manœuvred behind a Hun and fired, his superior performance enabled him to climb or dive to safety.

'Here's Ferrie!' cried someone. We followed his approach in silence, for no pilot, whatever he is doing, can resist watching a Pup
being landed. He didn't make a good three-pointer, in fact it was a
bumpy touchdown, and he ballooned a foot or so. When he taxied
in we discovered why. He'd been shot about, and his elevator controls
weren't functioning. He wasn't smiling so broadly as he usually does.
A burst had come in around his feet, without hitting him, but smashing against the base of the joystick, hence the unresponsive controls.
He'd come down from patrol very carefully, and then he'd missed
his way.

Led by Scott, we slouched in our sheepskin thigh-boots to the
squadron office at the end of the tarmac. We entered the office, or
rather crammed into it, for it was barely large enough to hold the
two desks of the major and the Recording Officer plus a filing cab-
inet and a safe. The major was out, and Captain Thompson, the R.O.,
which was just the active-service name for adjutant, drew a pad in
front of him, and looked at Scott expectantly.

But already everybody was chattering cheerfully, for apart from
the stimulation of the flight, we were still feeling the intoxicating effect of flying for two hours in the rare air of high altitudes, which
took some time to wear off, like alcohol.

'Be quiet, you rowdy devils!' cried the R.O. explosively. The hubbub subsided.

'Any luck, Nobby?' he asked Scott.

'We ran into eight D–IIIs, and were bloody lucky to be at 17,000, so we were able to make rings round them. Two or three down by my reckoning, but I've not checked up properly yet. One was mine, I reckon—I don't know who got the others. I saw mine, a red and black, start a spin, but only watched him a second—too many bullets around for Hun gazing. . .'

'Red and black?' I broke in. 'I saw him spinning—in fact he nearly hit me. I was just below you then, climbing up. The pilot's head was bent over against his gun-butts. I'm pretty sure he'd been hit.'

'Fine!' exclaimed Scott, pleased at this confirmation.

'All right, that's one D–III out of control to Captain Scott,' said Thompson, reading the line jotted on the pad. 'Next, please.'

'I fired at several others, but didn't see what happened to them,' said Scott. 'It was pretty fierce while it lasted. What did the rest of you do?'

The impatient pilots, too long suppressed, spoke out eagerly, and again their five voices burst into loud chorus.

'One at a time, *please!*' requested the R.O. in pained protest.

'I got about thirty rounds into a yellow and black striper, like a wasp,' began Courtneidge. 'He was on a Pup's tail . . .'

'That was me,' I exclaimed. 'I owe you a drink, Charles!'

'It's a pleasure,' grinned Courtneidge. 'But he didn't go down. I put another burst into a brown and white, at close range, he reared up, then I was fired on and I lost him . . .'

'I thought I saw a chunk rip away from a mottled greeny-grey chap while I was giving him a burst,' broke in Odell. 'It came off the front of his fuselage. I was hoping he'd break up, but he didn't, he went on turning.'

'Yes, I fired at that one too,' broke in Scott, 'but some silly idiot nearly bumped into me just as I'd got on his tail. . . .'

'Afraid that was me,' I admitted. 'Sorry, Skipper, I was being shot up after I'd put thirty rounds or so into the blue and white. He reared up and stalled sideways and dived away, but I didn't see whether . . .'

'The blue and white—the one with the long strut streamers!' exclaimed Eberlin. 'I saw him. He dived down nearly vertically, quite a way, but I only caught a glimpse. . . .'

'Anyone see the blue and white come up again?' asked Scott. 'He'd be the formation leader.'

Nobody could remember one way or the other.

'I rather think I saw him myself at the end,' said Scott. 'Maybe his guns had jammed.'

'I did see one spinning down well below,' interposed Courtneidge, 'but he was mostly yellow. I was turning and only got a glimpse, like Eberlin, and so I can't say. . . .'

'If only you'd send the bastards down in flames it would save all this argument,' complained Thompson. We laughed—we could take this sort of thing from him, for he wore the observer's wing, gained only on active service. 'Well, chaps, any more?'

'Half a minute, Tommy,' broke in Scott. 'This spinner Courtneidge saw. He wasn't the red and black that Lee confirmed for me—anyone have a shot at a yellow?'

'I did,' said Courtneidge, Ferrie and Eberlin together.

'I had a quick poop at him myself,' said Scott. 'Somebody must have hit him, but heaven knows who. . . .'

'All right, another down out of control, shared,' agreed the R.O. 'What next?'

'I put a good burst into another blue machine,' said Courtneidge. 'He had a red band around the fuselage. He skidded off sideways, and started a steep glide . . . anybody see him?'

'I spotted one going down steeply as the scrap finished,' broke in Ferrie, 'getting steeper and steeper. He was well below. I couldn't see its colour.'

'Maybe wounded,' commented Thompson. 'But under control. Nobody will get any thanks from Wing for that. Come on, chaps, keep moving, Wing are waiting for me to telephone all this.'

'I got behind a red and green,' I told him, 'and gave him twenty rounds, at fifty yards, but the wasp got behind me and I had to break off. . . .'

'I had a good scrap with a silver chap with black stripes along the wings,' said Ferrie. 'I'd have sworn I'd hit the pilot twice at close range but instead he nearly got me. Got a burst below my seat and hit the joystick and controls. The Pup's a write-off, I'm afraid, Scott— it's a 'C' Flight machine—two shots through the bottom port longeron.'

'Blast!' exclaimed Scott. 'That's a good Pup too. There were several Huns with red on them—that's Richtofen's mob's colour. Wonder if he was with them?'

'They were doing good shooting,' I said. 'They put two or three bursts into me. . .'

'Me too,' broke in Eberlin. 'I got about a dozen rounds through my top planes. . . .'

The others broke in with similar words—everyone had been winged.

'Nobby!' broke in Thompson, 'I'm not interested in what they did to you, I want to know what you did to them. Now, any more claims?'

'I suppose everybody got a few shots into one or more Huns,' commented Scott, 'but with no decisive result. From 17,000 you're just not able to watch whether they really go right down or whether they climb up again. Now, chaps, if that's the lot . . .'

'Wait a minute, Skipper,' said Eberlin, 'I did spot a Hun going down in a spin, too, but then he levelled out and I lost him. I didn't notice his colour much—a sort of mottled brown, I suppose.'

'That's mine!' cried Ferrie. 'I moved in close to him, shot off thirty rounds, then had to break off . . .'

'If he levelled out, he doesn't count,' pronounced the R.O., 'he was just getting out of your way—probably came back and took a pot at you a minute later. Lord, it's hot in here with all you sweaty types packed like sardines—and the stink of that whale grease on your faces! Why can't you wash it off before you come into my office? Thank God the major's out.'

'There were eight when they dived on us, and five when the scrap broke up,' stated Scott. 'So three of them went down and stayed down. We've got two out of control confirmed, but, Tommy, I reckon you ought to count the steep diver that Ferrie saw as out of control too. The pilot must have been hit or his engine . . .'

'All right, all right, anything for peace,' agreed Thompson, 'though I don't guarantee that Wing will accept it.'

'Anything else, chaps?' asked Scott, 'Well, that's three down out of control.'

'Yours is the only one I can definitely allot,' announced Thompson, 'the two others you'll have to divide between you—if you think it's worth while. You do? Righto! But for the rest—inconclusive combat.'

'That's the worst of these bloody free-for-alls,' complained Scott, 'everybody gets shot up and has narrow squeaks, or maybe gets hit, everybody shoots at several Huns, and maybe hits them, but you can't stop the fight to watch 'em crash, so there you are, there's nothing to it. We may have killed three Huns and crashed three D–IIIs—but nothing's proved, so—inconclusive combat. My sainted aunt, you're right, Tommy, it *is* pretty foul in this dog-kennel.'

'Glad you see my point,' responded the R.O. 'And now clear out, you noisy, disreputable lot, and leave me in peace while I phone Wing.

'And I'd like a combat report from you, Nobby, as soon as you can manage it.'

We slowly made our way back to the tarmac, and went to our machines. My rigger met me with a knowing grin.

'I found another burst, sir,' he informed me, and knelt down along-side the fuselage. I knelt by him and peered under to where he pointed. A foot behind the back of my seat was a group of five holes.

'Is this where they came in?' I asked.

'No, sir, where they came out. They came in from behind, further down the fuselage, by the fin. That's why I didn't spot them straight-away. If Jerry had come at you in a flatter attack, he'd have got you in the back.'

I reflected uneasily on this. Which Hun was it? I couldn't tell. Any one of those bursts from astern. . . .

'A miss is as good as a mile,' I observed. I felt that some remark was necessary, and this was the best I could think of.

'Not as close a miss as the ones that mucked up your fairing, sir, that was a narrow squeak if ever there was one.'

'I suppose it was.' But I didn't want to dwell too much on my luck. 'Any damage that matters?'

'I've opened up the fuselage—one bracing wire cut. The wings are all right. The fairing's messed up a bit, but nothing to worry about. I'll get everything fixed up right away, and the holes patched— you're on patrol again this afternoon.'

I thanked him, and went off to the flight office. Somehow, I drew an odd satisfaction from the fact that he seemed much more pleased with the scars of battle than I was.

ELEVEN
CLOUDED SKIES

My second show on that July Saturday was at four in the afternoon, a standby call, upon which Charles Courtneidge and I, the two next for duty, rushed from the squadron office to our Pups waiting on the tarmac, leapt into the air and made off south-eastwards towards La Bassée, climbing as we went. Our job was to chase away and if possible shoot down a German artillery two-seater supposed to be operating there at 5,000 feet, but, as usual, we were pursuing a ghost, for the E.A. had vanished.

Orders were that once in the air we had to complete a two-hour patrol, and Charles began to climb towards the flank of an immense mass of woolly cumulus, one of scores gliding across a clear blue sky. In weather such as this we found a certain enjoyment in being among so benign an array of vaporous monsters, with their gleaming white tops and billowing folds, all positioned at convenient distances from each other to allow us to hop from one to another, and to dodge archie, as we did now.

And they were, of course, a wonderfully flexible tactical factor in air fighting, for you could hide round their curves and in their valleys while stalking Huns unseen, then dash out and ambush them. You could dive into the mist if you were cornered, and so could the Hun, which was sometimes baffling. You could amuse yourself skylarking around the snowy pinnacles, diving into canyons and zooming up smooth sunlit slopes, skimming close to solid-looking cliffs, with your wing-tip well into the white wall rushing past at ninety miles an hour. But you had to remember that death lurked in every bosomy curve, no matter how dazzlingly beautiful, for some crafty Hun might be round the corner.

And this we found at 8,000 feet, for when rounding a massive bulge of our chosen cumulus, I saw six Albatroses a thousand feet above, going north. Fortunately they did not notice us, and Charles kept discreetly alongside the sheltering folds which here were intensely white, so like vast heaps of snow that I felt I could lean out of my cockpit and scrape up handfuls—and maybe play snowballs with Charles or, insane thought, with a Hun!

Leaving our cloud, we struck out eastwards across the open sky, climbing still, for we were only at 9,000 feet, well below our proper tactical height. As though by routine Charles made for the next cloud in the line, for these huge floating masses reaching to 12,000 feet and more seemed always to be placed carefully in serried parallel columns, like fleets of icebergs in orderly array. As we closed towards this new colossus, I was shaken to see eight more V-strutters suddenly appear in a loose formation from behind the topmost billowy curve, their wings glittering in the sun. They were coming in our direction, some 4,000 feet above, but were not keeping much of a lookout, and I thankfully watched them pass over the heads of two innocent Pups, not in the least anxious to be overwhelmed and slaughtered. I caught up Charles and pointed to them, but he put his thumb down and continued climbing eastwards, though what he was after I had no notion, except maybe trouble.

But I was glad to have the big cumulus nearby, for had the Albatroses attacked we could have swung into it. It was a kind of fastness to which we could run for shelter, just as the first cloud had helped us to avoid the attentions of archie merely by screening us from below. And now as we clung to the flanks of cloud number two, I realised an odd thing about these bulky isolated masses. From the earth below, you see and think of them as moving, but in the air, they seem solid and stationary, each one your particular world, round which your aeroplane revolves, the distant earth below being merely a slowly moving backcloth.

It was odd too how you developed almost an affection for these vast lumbering chunks of vapour, for apart from their impartial way of offering a hiding-place to foe as well as friend, they were almost always benevolent creatures. To this extent they had much more personality than all other cloud formations except nimbus and storm.

In the exclusive world of the fighter pilot flying underpowered, fragile machines that were so subject to unfavourable weather, clouds were both important and interesting. He knew them all. Because the Pup could fly at 20,000 feet he passed through the feathery white wisps of cirrus and the thin, milky sheets of cirro-stratus as well as the mackerel pattern of cirro-cumulus, but these were all characterless and seldom of tactical use. He flew round the closely packed globes of alto-cumulus, usually between 8,000 and 15,000 feet, and the strato-cumulus, which merged into ordinary cumulus, and whose tops ranged from 6,000 to 12,000, all of which fell into the category of those which were his favourites.

But then came the variations of nimbus, telling of rain sooner or later and these covered a wide spread, from the massy cumulo-nimbus, with their flat anvil tops, to the normal rain cloud, dark and shapeless with ragged edges, and then to storm and thunder formations. Only a few evenings before I and three others had a taste of this kind of weather. Even as we started there were splashes of rain, then formless nimbus spreading quickly over the sky, and when we reached 10,000 feet wide-spreading layers had rolled in beneath us and hidden the ground.

Denser masses then piled up ahead, blocking our set patrol beat, and rather than swing around them our leader, Asher, decided to go through. A heavy rain-cloud is unpleasant to fly in, for it is very dark and dank, the mist is thick, you can't see past your wing-tips, the engine roar rebounds in your ears, and everything in the cockpit drips with moisture. I had to lift my goggles to read the instruments. I couldn't see Asher, nor either of my other companions, Odell and Ferrie. And apart from these various tribulations, I knew how easily

I could fall into a spin if I failed to keep straight and level.

Ordinarily you keep on an even keel, both fore-and-aft and later-ally, by reference to the horizon, to which you continuously and un-consciously adjust the controls. In a cloud there is no horizon, and you use the air speed indicator for fore-and-aft checks—increased speed means you're going down, and vice versa—and the bubble, like a carpenter's level, a joke as an instrument, for lateral angles. Wind on the side of the face means you're side-slipping. You keep straight by holding to the bearing on your compass, but this is another joke, for the slightest jerk of the rudder sets it spinning, and it needs a longish spell of smooth, straight flying to settle down again—and this you can't do in a cloud.

On this occasion we passed through our cloud without trouble only to find ourselves caught in a long canyon between towering masses of storm-cloud. The rain poured down, spattering the wind-screen and blocking my forward view. It was both difficult and dan-gerous trying to keep formation contact. We banked round wispy, wraith-like shapes floating across the channel, while enormous arms of mist belched out and joined up above and below, trapping us in a vast gloomy cavern. Visibility was down to fifty yards, and when I put my head a couple of inches clear of the windscreen to try to see further, the 90 miles-an-hour raindrops smacked like pellets into my skin, so that all I could do was to look sideways and hope for the best. Had we run into a group of Huns, there would have been a nightmare of a fight.

The unhappy Pup was being tossed about like a cork in the tur-bulent cross-currents and the bumps from the black clouds, and its pained shudderings and the buffetings of the wings came through to my hands as sharp blows on the joystick. Without an instant's lull, I had to smother these jolts and judderings to keep control of the ma-chine. For we were now in the maw of a thunderstorm, with vast evil clouds reaching high above, and flashes of lightning shooting past us into the hidden darkness below. And without a break, rain poured down on me, into my open cockpit, until I was soaked through, lit-erally to the skin. At last Asher spotted a hole in the grim imprisoning walls and we slid through to the open, clear of the heart of the storm, and though still in heavy rain, I took it as a pleasure after what we had just gone through.

In contrast with such disconcerting nimbus experiences, it was understandable why the predictable well-behaved cumulus, almost always the partners of good weather, were our favourites. But even in their reassuring company, I was beginning to wonder when Charles would turn back westwards, for we were some five miles over and there was a strongish wind blowing us always further into Hunland. My doubts were settled a minute later, for he suddenly rocked his wings and pointed to yet another group of V-strutters, five of them, who were gambolling round the peaks of a majestic iceberg some 2,000 feet below and to our starboard. They seemed to be enjoying themselves so much, like a flock of gulls circling aimlessly over a Cornish harbour, that it seemed a pity to disturb them, especially as they were D–IIIs.

But Charles was in an aggressive mood, and he indicated by undulations of his right hand that we were going to do a dive and zoom attack. I swung out to his right flank and we dropped into a steep dive. From a distance it was difficult to get a bead on to any particular machine because of the way they were swirling around, but at last I was able to keep my Aldis on a blue and yellow Hun, going at an angle away from me, sufficiently long to give him a burst of thirty rounds. Then when barely fifty feet above them we levelled out and, zooming up under the impetus of the dive, rose some 300 feet.

Charles continued the climb as steeply as the Le Rhône would lift us, then banked over for another attack. As we went down, I was sorry to see that there were still five, which meant that our shooting had been off target, but as we dropped into our brief dive, I managed to get off nearly fifty rounds at two machines that came into my sights. Then as we once more zoomed up, and I swiftly scanned the skies, I had an unpleasant shock, for there, 2,000 feet above, was a group of black specks, diving directly for us—no doubt the formation we had seen half an hour earlier.

Courtneidge saw them too, signalled violently, banked sharply and led me straight into the swelling walls of the iceberg alongside which our little combat had taken place. Compared with going through a rainstorm cloud, to fly through a compact cumulus was almost fun. At one moment you're in clear sunshine, under a deep blue sky, charging at a solid-looking white cliff towering 3,000 feet above, making for a rainbow circle with the Pup's head-on silhouette in the centre. The next you're engulfed in grey mist, unable to see ahead, your eyes glued to your instruments, keeping straight and level. The mist is damp, the engine echoes, you wonder why you're taking so long to get through, then there's a soft lightness, and suddenly you burst into the glaring sunshine again.

But when I did go through this time, Courtneidge wasn't there. While I was circling, looking for him, thinking that maybe he'd fallen into a spin, a machine issued from where I'd just left. But it wasn't a Pup! It was a silver-coloured Albatros, who'd followed us through. He at once made for me, and we began to wheel, trying to get a bead on each other, but I soon found that although I could readily turn inside him, at the height we were at, 8,000 feet, he could climb more steeply on the turn, and then he'd bank over to try to pot me in a short dive. All I could do was to turn in under him.

It was then that I realised that this wasn't a D–III but something different, with a rounded fuselage and a better performance. Afterwards I found that it was the recently introduced D–V, which had a more powerful engine than the D–III, and an oval cross-section fuselage. The poor old Pup was no match for a D–III, and much less of one for this silver fish.

After three or four circlings without a chance to fire a shot, while he took snap bursts at me with his two Spandaus, I became worried, for I knew that if I couldn't beat him, he was sure to get me in the end. I had to escape somehow, and I was just about to drop into a spin and hope for the best, when the plane turned off and made towards the cloud. At first I couldn't believe it, then I saw that the pilot was leaning forward over his guns. They'd jammed! What wonderful luck! I instantly twisted behind and fired, edging the tracer along the fuselage towards him. For once I was excited, I was shouting: 'Got you, you bastard!' and just as the tracer seemed to be going right into his back—blank silence! My gun had jammed too! Then he vanished into the cloud.

Cursing with rage, I hammered at the cocking handle, and it went down at the first blow. One solitary dud had saved him. But I'd been lucky too, his was much the better plane, and I'd have been a goner or a prisoner. Looking still for Charles, I began to circle the cloud when suddenly, rounding a bulge, I saw three more Albatroses, 200 yards away, coming dead for me. In a split second I'd banked and dived once more into the sheltering cumulus.

Half a minute later, as I issued from the other side, I saw two more Huns 400 yards away, diving steeply after a spinning Pup. Charles! The white lines of tracer flashed down, and it looked all up with him, but I turned towards them on full engine, hosing both Huns in turn, an impossible shot, long range, big deflection, but after about 100 rounds one of them pulled level and turned east, so I could have winged him.

I'd fired some fifty rounds more at the second Albatros when my gun stopped, but now the handle was down, I'd run out of ammunition. I gave Charles up as lost, for the Hun was still on his tail. I turned west to come home, but there was no end to this surfeit of Huns, for the three I'd just dodged came round the cloud and made for me, and this time they were between it and me.

I swung south, and luck was with me still, for there, half a mile away were three F.E.2ds. I pelted towards them, fired a red light, pointed to the Huns, the leader pilot saw, waved, and they followed me back to the cloud. But by the time we reached it the Albatroses had vanished, upon which I felt a complete fool. I drew close, gave the washout, they waved in acknowledgement, and went on with their job. I thought, How I'd hate to fight in a pusher, sitting in a sort of open bath-tub, projecting out in front of the wings, exposed to wind and weather, just like the aged Rumpeties I learned to fly on. It gave me the shivers to think of it.

While all this was happening, my cloud, and by now I rather felt that it was mine, had moved a long way eastwards with the wind, and me with it. I was miles over Hunland, alone, with no ammunition, and at the dangerous height of 6,000, cold meat for the most inoffensive Hun. I flew west, slipping furtively from cloud to cloud and keeping ceaseless watch. Suddenly I noticed a machine going west 1,000 feet below me, and I dropped down cautiously after it. It was dark brown—had roundels—it was a Pup! I went closer, and there was Charles not in the least a goner. So we went home together. His gun had jammed at the critical moment, like mine, hence the spin. He was well shot about, but I was lucky, for I had only four bullet holes, all from the silver D–V. Charles didn't know I'd taken one of his attackers off his tail, and stood me a drink when I told him.

He was not at all pleased that our dive and zoom effort was a failure, for we should certainly have bagged a couple of Huns between us, and we both decided to have our Aldis sights checked up once more. We had a good laugh at the notion of two Pups trying to deal with so many Huns, and calculated we'd run across twenty-four of them all told. We would not have been laughing but for our kindly cumulus, but both reckoned we had thoroughly enjoyed our hide-and-seek among the clouds.

TWELVE

DOG-FIGHT

Ahead to the eastwards, as far as I could see in a careful search, there was still no other aeroplane in the sky, but away to the south-east I found a cluster of tiny dark specks glinting in the sun as they danced around the top slopes of a massive woolly-looking cloud. I counted them—four—five—or was it six?—no, there were five, on our level, and as I knew that the lynx-eyed Scott, our leader, would certainly have sighted them, I pigeon-holed their existence in my head, and gave my attention anew to keeping a lookout to our flanks.

We were on offensive patrol, four of us, and had flown five miles into Hunland, at 12,000 feet, a really unhappy tactical height for Pups, but one we were tied to because below us, at 8,000, were four Bristol Fighters from No. 11 Squadron. They were carrying out an important reconnaissance, about which we knew nothing, and although we were not an escort, as such, we had orders to keep over their heads, and to intervene if they were attacked.

It was an early autumn morning, and the sky was sparsely scattered with big, rounded mountains of dull grey cloud, lit only along their upper levels by a half-hearted sun filtering through a moisture-laden sky, and telling of bad weather to come. Below us, the ground was partly veiled in a soft mist which reached to the eastern horizon and concealed the secrets of Hunland in a pale obscurity.

Glancing southwards, I saw coming towards us a compact group of five objects which quickly took on the shape of aeroplanes, though not the usual biplanes, for they were Morane Parasols from No. 3 Squadron. From the front, in the air, they always seemed so odd with their single outstretched wing, the pylon centred above, and the fuselage and undercarriage dangling well below, looking for all the world like a sedge of herons about to touch down. They were a little higher than us, doing a close offensive patrol, and they soon slid behind us and disappeared. I thought of their pilots having to risk fighting Albatroses in those frail Blériot-type monoplanes, and knew that I was lucky to be flying Pups, out-dated though they were.

So far, except for the distant cluster, we had seen no enemy aeroplanes, and as we drove further into Hunland, the four of us invisibly tied together and moving as one, with nothing happening to occupy my thoughts, they ran idly on the question of who and what we should encounter this trip. Would we meet a big pack of D–IIIs or D–Vs and be overwhelmed, as had happened two or three times recently, and have to fight desperately just to preserve our skins? I wondered what my three companions were thinking of, whether in fact they were thinking of anything at all, which was the best condition for a fighter pilot.

When I first came to 46 Squadron, the excitement of being in the war and of fighting in the air absorbed me completely, but now that I was more sophisticated I had scope to wonder as we set out on each patrol whether we'd all come back. I'd think, Is this going to be my last flight? The thought would come briefly, and I'd touch wood and dismiss it, yet one couldn't always force it out of one's mind.

I'd been on active service long enough now to realise that one of my personal handicaps as a fighter pilot was that I had too vivid an imagination. Some of us, I concluded, had none at all, and were as insensitive and brave as a bull, their minds never dwelling for a moment on their risks. For such fortunate people, heroism came easily, but the ones with too lively an imagination were inflicted with a double restraint—first awareness not that they might die but of *how* they might die, and second the strain, not of passively accepting dan-

Albatros D-III (with D-V rudder) over Comines, 1918

Above: Fokker Triplane
taking off
Left: Fokker D–II
Below: Camel of 46
Squadron, Izel le Hameau

ger but of aggressively seeking it. But again these moments didn't last long, I was young and a little scatter-brained, and my mind quickly turned to the job in hand.

And not too soon, for there ahead were more specks, five of them, probably those I had pigeon-holed away. They were coming towards us from the south-east, some 2,000 feet above, and I knew exactly what was about to happen with two small formations such as we were—there would be a nasty close-in dog-fight, especially as they were Albatros D–IIIs, as I could now see. Absently I eased my fingers from the glove mittens, which I fastened, first one then the other, to the back of my wrist with the snap button. When the scrap started, I should need the full use of my fingers.

Since my arrival in France over four months ago, formation tactics had changed, for whereas we used to go on line patrol in pairs, now, except for standby chases of two-seaters, there were always at least four of us, usually five or six, and for D.O.P.s and sweeps, formations of two or three full flights were the normal, often with flights of Bristols below us, as in this present show. This change had come about partly because the Germans, led by Richtofen, had expanded the size of their formations, and we'd had to follow.

But the difficulty about these large groups of machines was that they couldn't be tactically handled in combat, for there was no way of control other than rocking wings, waving arms and firing Very lights, and these were only practicable before the action started. The result was that when two large formations of a dozen or more on each side tried to fight, they couldn't. They became two separate flocks of planes wheeling, climbing, diving, rushing forward to fire a burst then withdrawing, half-engaging then disengaging, singly or in pairs or even threes, but never in my experience to date wholly intermingling in one big battle.

Instead the opposing groups expanded upwards and to the flanks, seeking height and space to get to grips with the enemy, with flight leaders eventually losing even contact with their pilots. In this confusion, there was the ever present risk of passing across the fire of one's fellow pilots or even of colliding with their machines. The even greater danger to the too audacious pilot, or section of pilots, who dashed forward to make snap forays at close quarters was of going fifty yards too far, and being immediately overwhelmed, as had recently happened to a 46 Squadron pilot. In consequence of such drawbacks, the usual result of these confrontations was that we fired at each other at long range and sometimes scored a hit, then after twenty or thirty minutes of futile stone-throwing, the two fleets broke off and went home.

Real in-fighting took place only when the opposing groups were small, of average flight strength, with four to six on each side, and then a close mêlée could take place, fierce, brief and usually lethal, especially when numbers were equal and opposing planes paired off to fight what were in effect personal duels.

The course of such encounters was almost always the same. If one formation was higher than the other, it had the tactical advantage to choose when and how to attack. What followed was routine. We'd be in a reasonably tidy, though loose, formation, as also the Hun, and there'd be cohesion up to the dive, but then, under the stream of bullets, the formation being attacked was forced to split up and start wheeling erratically to avoid presenting sitting targets. The attackers had to split up too in order to follow their swerving targets. The situation was similar when formations met on the same level.

Once the combat was joined the leaders could hope for no tactical cohesion, for the fighting became at once a free-for-all, where each pilot was on his own, a fleeting target seeking enemy fleeting targets, reacting instantly to every change of situation in a wild affray of split-second escapes and opportunities, the whole game played with such ferocious pace and intensity that it was usually over within a few minutes.

And now, as there were only five of the enemy and four of us— for the Bristols were too far below to count unless the fight dragged on—there'd be a real dog-fight, and because the D–IIIs had the advantage in both numbers and performance, I faced the next few minutes with no great confidence, my one sheet anchor being the Pup's prodigious manœuvrability.

As the moment arrives, Scott fires a few shots to ensure that his Vickers is working, and as I edge off to the flank, I do the same. I am trembling with suspense and excitement, I feel my muscles grow tense, my fingers tighten automatically on the joystick control. The Huns are still hovering above us. Scott rocks his wings warningly, then, as their noses dip, waves his left arm as signal to break up, and himself turns off left. My eyes never leave the enemy. I gaze fascinated as five double lines of tracer stab down like straight white threads, and instinctively start a rapid turn to the right. They are five, we are four, three of us will pair off, but the fourth will have to deal with two of them.

The dive steepens, the Huns spread out, tracer still coming down at us in bursts, and then I see that two lines are converging upon me. So I am to be the unlucky one! Now that it has started, I am quite calm, still circling, trying to dodge their tracer, waiting for them to come down to my level. I don't dodge well enough, for a burst goes through my port wings, top and bottom, I see the holes suddenly appear.

Then it begins. Suddenly everyone is turning, swinging, zooming, skidding, and firing in short bursts at speeding targets. All of us, friends and enemies, know what we are doing, we are fairly seasoned fighters. I hear *crack-ak-ak-ak* from behind, the bullets are close, I smell the tracer and, good God, I see the flash of twin Spandaus reflected in my mirror. He's too close, he can't miss! I kick the right rudder, skid away in a flat turn, the crackle ceases, he roars over me, pale blue, a pretty machine, but he can't turn as quickly as the Pup.

How could he have missed me at that distance, less than eighty yards? Fourteen bullets a second, how could he miss? More cracks of passing bullets, the other Hun is taking his turn, angle shots, bullets smash into my dashboard, the compass bursts, the spirit splashes on to my knees. I see him out of the corner of my eye, along to my right, fifty yards away, grey fuselage, green wings, I see the sun glint on his goggles, he's staring at me as if he's expecting me to burst into flames at any moment.

I turn and turn frantically as they draw away and come back again.

Tracers flash past me, from behind, close alongside me, but only in the briefest of bursts, my twists and turns are baffling them so far. I haven't a hope of getting a shot at them, if I tie myself to one, the other will have me cold. Suddenly the Pup dips heavily—I have flown through somebody's slipstream. A black-and-white Hun, like a checker-board, streaks across my front and I give him a burst, a tricky shot, not a hope, but he's carrying the leader's long red streamers from his struts, so he's worth trying for.

The firing from behind has stopped. Have I got clear? I daren't turn to look. All around me machines are gyrating at over a hundred miles an hour, Pups and Albatroses, in an amazingly small aerial arena, rising, falling, banking vertically, missing each other by yards, tracer scratching the air between them, and yet nobody's been downed yet. It's the same old situation, Albatroses and Pups, the pigeons can't catch the sparrows and the sparrows can't hurt the pigeons. I wade in among them, putting blip bursts into any coloured plane that comes in front of me, thinking I've shaken off my two bastards, but suddenly the *crack-ak-ak-ak* starts again, tracer smokes past me from port astern.

Then more tracer from the other side. I zoom up violently, the pressure pushes me into my seat, my sight goes for a second, then more shots, they're both at me, I'm skidding madly, zooming, doing flat turns, quick rolls, anything to stop them getting a bead on me, throwing the poor old Pup around, my gentle sensitive Pup, her startled shudders of protest almost hurt, but there's no smooth flying in a shambles like this, it's ham-fisted stuff or you're out. And it's just as hard on the engine, open throttle the whole time, going full out, roaring in protest, propeller racing, bracing wires screaming.

I've had enough already, but I've got to keep up this wild split-assing if I want to stay alive. I'm right about this, for a sudden burst comes from behind, the bullets smash into the top centre section, I swing up and over on to my back in a half-roll, and there just beneath me is the blue Hun, who was doing the firing, he's caught me up and he's a yard below. I cringe into my seat, my heart stops, his too, for he drops away violently. The Pup's still upside down, I'm hanging on my belt, then, when I come off the half-roll I'm too shaken to go after him, in fact I feel sick. Dog-fights are made up of split-second incidents, and they stick in the memory, like snap-shots in the mind, and this last one I'll remember for ever.

Crack-ak-ak-ak, the other devil's after me, and, Christ, I'm flying straight, the one suicidal sin in a dog-fight. I skid off to the right, if it's not one it's the other, I'm trapped, I'm desperate, if there's no escape and I've got to be done in I'll ram one of them—grey-green swings off to the left, trying to turn after me, but the Albatros just won't come round that quickly. Then *rak-ak-ak* again, the blue one has come back, I skid once more to the right, but I'm wasting my time, I'll never get out of this.

I'm fighting this ruddy war on my own. I've had it before in other scraps, surrounded by hurtling planes, but alone, fighting a battle on my own. It's every man for himself, everybody's too busy avoiding bullets and trying to get a snatched burst into a Hun, no time to think of the other Pups. But Scott is different, he does find time, he comes zooming up behind the blue, who's too intent on getting on my tail to look after his own.

In his first burst Scott hits him in a vital spot. He's a damned good shot, Nobby. All in a flash I see the Hun dip his nose and dive down vertically, with Scott after him, gun going. No good, little boy blue, I croak exultantly, Nobby's got you, bullets go quicker than diving Albatroses—they'll soon catch you up!

Then I come to and look around, on the turn, always on the turn. The relief to be rid of that blue bastard! But where's the grey-green? Other Huns whirl around, and Pups, tracers are criss-crossing, hanging momentarily in the air. Bullets are cracking past me from somewhere—silly if I flew into a burst meant for somebody else! What a thrilling, ridiculous business it all is.

More bullets crack past my ears, more stinking tracer, coming from three-quarters astern, the grey-green is still after me, he seems set on sending me down. Why *me!?* I bank vertically right, yanking the stick back into my belly, then swing after him as he rushes behind, bully the Pup again fiercely to get him in my sights. I fire, the tracer flashes into his fuselage, I hose it towards the pilot, but he pulls up and away. That's where their big Mercedes engine comes in, they can *climb* out of trouble.

He pulls round in a wide curve behind me, and it begins all over again, I start turning, he comes down on my tail, firing short bursts, but they miss me, we're now circling round each other on the same level, duelling, I tighten my turn, pull behind him, open fire, the tracers seem to go into the engine, he pulls up again, banks round, then comes at me from ahead to port. The two Spandaus flash at me, but I'm already skidding off, and then, appearing from nowhere, Courtneidge, he's behind the Hun, on his tail as they pass over me. I see Courtneidge's tracer going in from thirty yards' range. The grey-green pulls up steeply, falls over sideways, and drops down, with the Pup after him, gun going.

I draw a deep breath. My mouth is dry and I wet my lips, my heart is thumping. Where are the others? I see Scott circling with the checkered Hun a hundred yards away. A Pup suddenly pulls over from the left, number five, Odell, he's hitting at his cocking handle with the hammer—a jam—then he's disappeared. Bullets are coming up from beneath, I look down and see the Bristols, they have climbed up, one much higher than the rest. Now they're near enough for the observers to fire, which they couldn't before for fear of hitting us. There are two more Huns somewhere, and as I swing round to make sure they're not behind me, I see them. One is being fired at by the highest Bristol, it's attacking him from a flank.

But the other is coming in from the south, two hundred yards from me, and is curving round to attack the Bristol from the rear. The other Bristols are pooping at him but their tracers are going wide. I have height, I start a steepish dive and as the Hun drops down in a right hand turn behind the Bristol to come up from under, I slide in after him on the impetus of my dive.

At the last second he sees me and tries to pull clear, but makes the fatal mistake of doing an S-turn, which puts me right on his tail, and because I've cut the bend I'm only thirty yards behind, and can hardly miss. I give him three good bursts, he rears up almost vertically, nearly hitting the Bristol's tail unit, hangs on his prop stalling for three or four seconds, then falls over sideways into a spin. I don't watch, this can be fatal with other Huns about.

I glanced round. The two remaining Huns had fled, hotly pursued by a couple of Bristols. I saw two Pups. Now I could look for my Hun. For several seconds I couldn't find him, then suddenly I spotted him, still slowly spinning. This could be a ruse to get away, I've done it myself, but no, he was going round with that uneven, flicking movement which spelt an uncontrolled spin. I watched him intently as his wings glinted in the sun at each turn. He was taking a long time to go down, sliding sometimes slantwise like a falling leaf, then going on to the vertical again. Suddenly he seemed to melt away. He'd dropped into the layer of mist and I was robbed of the pleasure of seeing him crash.

Suddenly Scott fired a red Very light, and we rallied on him, and resumed our patrol, for the Bristols hadn't yet completed their re-connaissance. They dropped down to 8,000 feet again and we trailed into Hunland for another twenty minutes before turning for home. We met no more Huns, which was fortunate, for we'd used up most of our ammunition, except Odell, who'd had a succession of jams.

Back at the aerodrome, we sorted out our scores. Scott had sent the blue one down completely out of control, I'd sent down mine ditto, but in a spin, confirmed by the observer of the first Bristol, while Courtneidge could only claim a 'driven down' because he had no chance to watch it falling, for another Hun attacked him from behind at the critical moment. In this fight, the way it worked out, it was simple enough to decide who should have credit, but that didn't often happen in a dog-fight.

First you could seldom be sure whether the machine you'd sent down was a certainty unless it broke up or burst into flames, for in a wild free-for-all you just couldn't watch it to the ground. Second, in a real rough house, with half a dozen machines shooting in short bursts at any Hun, it was sometimes impossible to say for certain who put *finis* to even a flamer or a break-up. Third, there was the compli-cation that the Hun who dropped away in what seemed a death dive might level out lower down when he was safe, whereas a machine that dropped out of the fight apparently under full control might have a mortally wounded pilot with just enough strength to reach his aerodrome. The Huns had the advantage that nine-tenths of the fighting took place over their side of the Lines, and thus they had evidence of every British machine that crashed or was forced to land, or that went down through engine failure or a wounded pilot.

My poor old Pup was a write-off. Twenty-eight bullet-holes, two main spans smashed, plus the dashboard and compass and rear centre section struts. But not a shot touched me. I suppose I'm lucky.

THIRTEEN

THE ABODE OF LOVE

The Abode of Love, the best-known Nissen in France, was set in Paradise—a miniature paradise in the orchard of an old mansion, once a château, but now Filescamp Farm, which stood in open countryside near the smiling little village of Izel le Hameau, some ten miles west of Arras.

The farm and its outbuildings and the large orchard lay on a tree-sheltered slope immediately below a veritable tableland topping the 120-metre contour line, which was the immense, level aerodrome. On its flanks was permanent accommodation for three squadrons, and there was ample room for double that number.

In the earlier years the aerodrome had been occupied by the French air services, but after the British front was extended southwards, a succession of Royal Flying Corps squadrons was stationed there in varying strength, the concentration during the Battle of Arras in April and May 1917 being Nos 11, 29, 60 and 100 Squadrons, as well as the 13th Wing at Izel.

Many stout-hearted airmen had gone aloft from Izel le Hameau, some of whom won fame and honour among the top-scoring aces. Ball, McCudden and Bishop had all flown and fought from there, but the first two never knew the Abode of Love, which came into being after Ball's time with 60 Squadron around August 1916, and McCudden's time with 29 Squadron from October of the same year.

McCudden was then a sergeant pilot, flying D.H.2s, on which he was fortunate to survive the unit's routine combats with Boelcke's Staffel equipped with the Halberstadt and the Albatros D–I and D–II. Thus far the Canadian Billy Bishop had been the outstanding fighter ace operating from Izel, but he was to be closely followed in late 1917 and in 1918 by another Canadian, Don MacLaren, and by the Scot, George Thompson, both of 46 Squadron.

The Abode of Love began as the normal half-barrel-shaped Nissen hut divided into four cubicles, one of a group erected by a company of Royal Engineers for 60 Squadron when the unit moved to Izel, for the second time, in December 1916. Stirred to their best by the squadron's thrustful C.O., Major E. P. Groves, they built a comfortable Officers' Mess with a large brick fireplace, a similar Mess for the sergeants, who also had Nissens to live in, and above-average accommodation for the other ranks. Later, in April, the squadron constructed a hard tennis court in the orchard, using stone from the mines at Bruay.

In June the three flight commanders of 60, one of whom was Bishop, discovered that they did not like the cramped cubicles and, deciding to join up in one large room, selected a Nissen opposite the Mess, and had the cubicle partitions removed. There was then sufficient space to have tables and chairs for a game of cards or other sociable activities not always feasible in a noisy, crowded Mess. But their move evoked mocking gestures from some of the other pilots, who began by painting 'Saloon Bar' on a filled-in window space, and followed this up with 'Hôtel du Commerce' under the rounding edge of the corrugated-iron roof. Finally some more gifted wag painted 'Abode of Love' on the door, and so the hut became and remained always the Abode of Love.

From then on, with 60 Squadron's pilots as for those of 46 after we took over the cantonment at the beginning of September, when they reluctantly exchanged their comfortable living quarters for the muddy tents we had vacated at St Marie Cappelle, the Abode was the backdrop of the lighter side of Mess life. Facing the entrance of the long Mess hutment of which it became almost an extension, the space between them was where we congregated in fine weather for drinks, or just to stand in the sun, or where we placed tables for poker or bridge, and inevitably where we took snapshots, almost all group photographs having the Abode as background.

The occupants of the Abode never had great privacy, for it was the one dwelling that we all entered at some time or other, especially in bad weather, or when evening binges spilled over from the ante-room. They shared their hut with other occupants too. During 60 Squadron's reign the Abode was the home not only of the three captains but of the unit's two senior pet mongrels, and similarly, during the time of 46, although the Abode was not then confined to flight commanders, our top-level pet Jock, a black Scots terrier, conde-scended to make it his principal residence.

The farm itself, owned by the ubiquitous and long-suffering Monsieur Tetus, was a handsome old building with high grey walls enclosing a large courtyard centred by a pond. Here were geese, ducks, chickens, flocks of pigeons, scores of caged rabbits, and nu-merous pens crammed with pigs of all sorts and sizes. Although to have this farmyard collection next door was both interesting and amusing at times, it was also a nuisance, for the mosquitoes were high-powered beasts, and the place was infested with large rats which did not seem to realise they had no right to prowl round our messes and hutments. To keep them down we had to organise periodical massacres, using Very cartridges to drive them from their holes into the waiting jaws of the full assembly of the squadron's canine popu-lation, drawn from the officers', sergeants' and men's messes.

Occasionally we had exciting interludes when a cohort of pigs es-caped their pens and raided the orchard for fallen fruit. They were smelly, hefty and obstinate, and readily became aggressive when we tried to induce them to return to their own ground, and our only remedy then was to withdraw with dignity and go for a walk.

The great joy of the rural situation of the Mess was the orchard, for here in the hot weather we could sit in the shade with the light breeze rustling through the branches, and all was peace except for the mosquitoes and the wasps. In theory the fruit was the property of Monsieur Tetus, but as it was always right in front of us, there for the taking, there was seldom much of a crop for his workers to collect.

On a fine September afternoon, to sit among the trees, their leaves filtering the sun as one took a nap after a bountiful lunch, was indeed the height of contentment. From our seats between the Mess and the Abode and other huts we couldn't even see the hangars at the top of the slope. We were far, far away from all the ugliness of war, especially the war of the trenches.

When 60 Squadron had to surrender their much prized Mess they quite reasonably stripped it of everything moveable, and as we possessed only a piano, a ping-pong table and a few decrepit chairs, the ante-room was a squalid sight on our opening day of occupation. At a Mess meeting held that same evening some of the more extravagant types wanted to refurnish *de luxe*, at a cost of ten pounds or more a head, but as I was saving up for leave, I protested. We did not need a Palm Court lounge so long as we were comfortable, I said, and what was the use of buying expensive French furniture just to smash it up on a binge night? Some of the company, headed by Shadwell, agreed with me, and a vote was taken, but before I could realise my danger a resolution was proposed which landed Shadwell and me with the job of making the place shipshape on as little money as possible. The resolution was passed unanimously, and with rude comments at that, because Shadwell and I were the only two out of all the pilots who were married.

Next day, in between patrols, he and I began listing out the items of furniture and equipment needed, a lengthy business, but our most urgent needs were comfortable armchairs and a stock of second-rate chairs for binge parties to vent their high spirits on. We then drove to Doullens and filled the tender with a load from secondhand shops, in a series of transactions which mysteriously left us fifty francs down, a loss we philosophically shared.

The next step was to send for the corporal carpenter and ask him to get busy on our proposed structural improvement, of which the most pressing was a bar, but he pointed out that he had no wood. I obtained a Crossley, and resisting the temptation of the unoccupied camp buildings immediately next to our own, drove to the equally empty quarters for a squadron at the western end of the aerodrome. Here we borrowed a satisfactory collection of suitable loot.

The bar, complete with footrail, was installed within twenty-four hours, as well as such extras as a mantelshelf, bookshelves and fireside seats, for 60 had kindly abstained from taking the brick fireplace with them. The seats were for us to make our own toast with the long forks which I provided. We also aspired to a more civilised bath-house than the hole in the ground which 60 had left, and contrived a stand-up shower in which, by gently pulling a rope, we tipped over a couple of buckets of hot water suspended above while we stood on a duck-board over a drainage pit. As soon as this was in use, the carpenter called on me to devise a grease box for straining the overflow from the pit, which was fouling a slice of the orchard.

Within a few days Shadwell managed to get himself shot down, and some time elapsed before we learned that he was a prisoner of war. Meanwhile I had to continue with refurbishing the Mess on my own, as nobody could be persuaded to offer a hand. After having the mess-room and ante-room whitewashed, the walls and floors nicely stained, new curtains fitted, the kitchen enlarged, the bar and other fitments fixed, and the furniture put in place, I thought I could wash my hands of the whole business. But Major Babington had different ideas.

First he wanted me to have some more stain made up for him to take to Wing and this I did, then he asked me to produce a to-scale sketch of the fireside seats, which I also did. I was somewhat taken aback when he then asked me to buy a young pig from Monsieur Tetus, again for Wing, not as a pet but to eat. After carrying out this unexpected duty, I firmly resigned from my one-man spare-time band.

The only gain to me for all my labours was the luxury of an elec-tric light over the bed in my cubicle. Because Filescamp was nowhere near a town supply of electricity, we had to produce our own current on sets which serviced the workshops and hangars and the three messes. Any overload quickly caused trouble, and thus our cubicle lighting was by smelly, smoky oil lamps. But an extension which I fixed up for the major's hut, and to forestall envious comment, extended to the flight commanders' cabins, somehow had to be routed by way of mine.

The Mess, which was small, as we were only eighteen pilots plus the C.O. and the Recording, Gunnery and Equipment Officers, at once became a comfortable and friendly place, with the Abode as practically an additional ante-room. We were indeed fortunate to possess the tennis court, and a badminton court in an empty hangar next door, as well as the much-used ping-pong table in the mess room. The only recreation we lacked, and we were aware of it because of the fun we'd had in the River Lys at La Gorgue, was somewhere to swim, but we were too high up for any sort of river to run within miles.

We realised our good fortune whenever we visited neighbouring squadrons, such as 3 at Warloy, Naval 8 at St Eloi or 11 at Bellevue, none of which had our club-like atmosphere, especially the last, because it was a two-seater squadron, with double our officer strength. But much the most salutary lesson in counting our blessings was to visit the Pilot's Pool Mess at No. 2 Aircraft Depot at Candas, near Doullens, where we had to go when collecting new machines.

My worst experience there was when with Odell and Armitage I set off by Crossley one morning to fetch three new Pups, but after we'd been on the road for most of the three-hour journey, the weather changed, low clouds rolled up, and by the time we arrived they were down to the ground. I decided to stay on, expecting that conditions might improve in the afternoon.

Nonentities such as us types from the front-line squadrons were not allowed to set foot in the Depot's Staff Mess and so we went to the Pool, where we had the unappetizing lunch which was the normal, as for some inexplicable reason this Mess took a pride in consistently providing the worst food I'd known during my army service, which was saying something. Hoping that the weather would yet clear, we spent an hour or two in the bare, frowsty ante-room, yarning with the new arrivals in the Pool, just from England, awaiting their turn for posting. Then we tried the tea, which tasted of soapsuds and was accompanied by pink dog biscuits.

By now it was raining, and we were committed to stay the night, but with rueful thoughts about our own cosy Mess, decided we could not face an evening in the Pool, and drove to Doullens, where after visiting a cinema, we enjoyed a good dinner, with three bottles of wine, at the Quatre Fils. Returning to the Pool, we found that there were no spare beds, so we borrowed blankets and coats and tried to sleep in our flying kit on the concrete floor in a Nissen hut. In spite of the din made by a party of well-primed Pool pilots next door, who were doing a non-stop concert with a piano, drums, cornets, rattles, whistles and loud yells—and I couldn't blame them, living in this miserable hole—the wine quickly sent us off.

We were up at dawn, and paid one-and-eightpence each for the privilege of refusing a cup of tepid tea tasting this time of fish, with no milk or sugar, and with more dog biscuits, but now brown and mouldy. This so-called breakfast was served in a dirty cold flapping tent, with the atmosphere of a morgue. The weather was still bad, but it would have had to be far worse to keep us another unnecessary minute at Candas. After some delay caused by damp magnetos, we started off, flying at fifty feet, but before long the clouds lifted to 100 and then to 500, and we finished the seventy-mile journey without trouble. As soon as we landed, without wasting a second, we hastened down to the Mess for a decent breakfast, never for a moment ceasing to thank our lucky stars that we were not stationed at Candas.

Compared with squadrons situated within walking distance of towns like Bailleul and Bruay, with shops, cinemas, cafés, clubs and bawdy houses, our one hardship at Filescamp was that it was isolated, being two miles from even a main road, and apart from Arras, which was a ruin, and Avesnes le Comte, which was no more than an over-grown village, the nearest towns, St Pol and Doullens, were twelve and fifteen miles distant. We could often get a lift into Avesnes, and even to St Pol, because tenders ran there most days on shopping ex-peditions for the messes, while there were fairly frequent runs to

Doullens on visits to the Depot.

But to go further afield, which meant Amiens, about thirty-five miles away, some important reason for the journey was essential, and the usual pretext was that the workshop urgently needed a carborundum wheel. Why Amiens was officially acceptable as the one place to buy carborundum wheels I never fathomed. To us Amiens was the big city, with all the trimmings of a civilised life, especially a good restaurant, the Godbert, whose *filet de sole* was alone worth the long ride in a bumpy Crossley. To some visitors, Amiens had the special advantage of possessing, in addition to the too-popular Number Ten, a selection of other officers' licenced brothels, which was a real advance on the monopolistic situation in the smaller towns.

Because of the time involved in reaching sizable centres, a pilot could usually only joy-ride to them on his weekly day off, and so most of us tended to stay put in our orchard and Mess. Outdoors, in addition to tennis and badminton and in good weather, ping-pong, there was gardening for those who liked it, on the beds of flowers between the Mess and the Abode and outside the other huts, for which plants and seeds were brought from England. There were pleasant walks across open fields to the villages around, seemingly untroubled by war except for the lack of men for labour, the prettiest village being Izel le Hameau itself, in whose cemetery we buried those of the squadron who died in local crashes or of wounds.

Apart from exercise, many of us had something besides reading and cards to occupy our free hours. For the musically inclined there was the piano and the gramophone in the ante-room, and a few of us had portable gramophones in our cabins, with selections of classical records that provided a counter-blast to the London show hits that blared away interminably. Others among us had special interests, such as me with my writing, Courtneidge with his clever sketches, and the major with his silhouette portraiture. He sat you sideways in darkness with a candle on one side of your face and a sheet of paper, pinned to a board, on the other, then deftly pencilled your profile and head and blacked it in afterwards.

The abiding friendliness of the Mess was something that most of

Some pilots of 46 Squadron. *Above left:* Denham Jenkins *Above right:* Robin-son (Chockololovich) *Below left:* Cooper (Hootsmon) *Below right:* Dimmock and Scott in cheerful mood on posting to H.E.

Above: Nieuport two-seater of 46 Squadron. The deputy-leader pilot waves
to the photographing aeroplane
Below: L.V.G C-II (C443)

us took for granted, but to me, who had known other Messes where the junior newcomer was received by the older members if not with hostility at least with indifference, and where several days might pass before he could even begin to feel that he belonged, it was surprising how quickly new arrivals entered into the close circle of the Izel Mess.

Casualties at the start of September and postings to Home Establishment of some of our veteran pilots had brought a steady succession of replacements, but in the atmosphere of our light-hearted, enlivening community they soon found their feet. Then, after one good binge night, they usually woke up next morning feeling firmly ensconced as members of 46.

One such binge was held towards the end of September to celebrate 'C' Flight's effort in bringing down four Huns that day, an Albatros scout each to Scott, Courtneidge and me, and a two-seater Albatros shared between the three of us. This was the first real carouse since my essay into interior decoration, and I had almost the feeling of being host in a restaurant. After the usual rowdy dinner we sang the squadron ballads, with Normie Dimmock rolling out the old familiar melodies on our battered piano.

Never could we get through a sing-song without the ritual Flying Corps ditties of woe, of which the following were among the easiest to chorus:

> Wrap me up in my old yellow jacket,
> Give me my joystick to hold, to hold,
> Let me fly once again o'er the trenches,
> Thus shall my exploits be told, be told.
> *and*
> The young aviator lay dying,
> And as in the wreckage he lay,
> The mechanics all gathered around him
> To carry the fragments away.
> *and*
> He was diving at the Hun

At two hundred miles an hour
When his wing tore off like a leaf.
They found him in the wreck,
With his hand upon the throttle.
He was butchered beyond belief, beyond belief.
He was diving at the Hun
Which he'll never do no more
'Cos he was butchered beyond belief, beyond belief.

These dirge-like doggerels were a mock-heroic rejection of fear, a maudlin scoffing at mortality, a reduction of gory extinction to the level of nursery rhymes, yet they were sung as lustily by veterans who had seen sudden death, and escaped by inches, as they were by novices from England, to whom a violent end by bullets was still entirely an abstraction.

From these verses we passed to others slightly less lugubrious such as 'We Haven't Got a Hope in the Morning', 'The Only, Only Way', 'Who Killed Cock Robin?', Heavy-Handed Hans', and the always popular 'So Early in the Morning':

The orderly bloke was asleep in bed,
He woke up with a splitting head,
The telephone bell began to ring,
More hot air from the Thirteenth Wing.
So early in the morning, so early in the morning,
So early in the mooor-ning,
Before the break of day.
The orderly officer said 'Who's that?'
The Wing replied, 'There's a Halberstadt
Right over Arras so they say,—
Go and drive the bugger away!'
So early in the morning . . . .

Another which chorused very well was 'The Syncopated Fire Control'.

In single-seater Sopwith Pups
You're always on the top
With a synchronising fire control
So you can't hit your prop.
Oh! that syncopated fire control
Very fascinating on the whole
To hear your gun go Pop! Pop! Pop!
'Till crash! you've shot off your prop!
It's not a matter for chatter,
You're up the pole!
Damn that syncopated fire control!

No sing-song was complete without hits from the London shows, and we usually managed to include such favourites as: 'If You were the Only Girl in the World', 'Here Comes Tootsie, Play a Little Music on the Band', 'Hello my Dearie, I'm Lonesome for You', 'Sister Susie's Sewing Shirts for Soldiers', 'Every Little While I Feel so Lonesome', 'Some Girl has got to Darn his Socks', and the tuneful 'Husband and Wives, think of their lives, always together, in every kind of weather'.

After we had exhausted ourselves shouting our heads off, and Dimmock was wilting with fatigue, and even the piano was creakingly complaining, the party took on a riotous mood, with the more tipsy types smashing things, at which I was gratified to see how useful was my stock of expendable chairs. There were scuffles and free fights and broken bottles and shattered glasses, and one pilot fractured a bone in his foot trying to vault into the bar, and next day was duly carted to the Casualty Clearing Station at Agnez. A couple of the more plastered revellers had to be carried forcibly to bed after trying with hoots of laughter to demolish everything movable, including our precious gramophone.

By then nearly a quarter of our strength had drifted over to the Abode of Love, where with fresh supplies of beer and whisky we found our second wind and started all over again, until once more a couple of the more inebriated enthusiasts wanted to break up the tables and chairs, which didn't amuse the owners at all. To wreck things in the Mess was one thing, they were public property, but to despoil the Abode of Love ... we all agreed and bundled the offenders out. After which somebody produced a mouth-organ, and we began another round of chanties which went on until its owner fell asleep while playing.

This particular party did much to consolidate us all, veterans and new hands, into a tight friendly group, and this was essential if we were to do our job efficiently. As members of a team, we had to have a good understanding with each other. It was inevitable that because of our isolation and because we could not be for ever dashing out of camp after girls, wives and relations, as in England, we were thrown very closely together, every day, every evening. Over and above this communal life in the Mess, we were linked by the comradeship of hazards shared in the air.

Yet strangely, with few exceptions, we did not get to know each other with deep intimacy. We did not often talk about our past, for we were too young to have a past, nor about our future, for we could not visualise a future other than as a continuation of the present. One knew little or nothing about the next fellow's background, whether he was rich or poor, well born or lowly born, intellectual or ignorant, for these did not count. All that counted was what he did in the air.

We did distinguish the 'coloured troops' from the rest of us, for that was the label given to Canadians, Australians, Rhodesians and all the other pilots from the Colonies, but there were so many of them, especially of Canadians, who at times, in some squadrons, outnumbered every other breed of British, that eventually we all settled down to the same level of near anonymity.

Our interests, however diverse our backgrounds, whether we were 'white' troops or 'coloured', whether we were artistically-minded like Courtneidge, or mechanically-minded like Bulman, or girl-minded like every other one of us, all eventually centred on our job, which reduced to its essence was to dash out periodically from the secluded world of Filescamp Farm, leap into the air to try to slay a few Germans, then return gratefully to the home comforts of the orchard and the Mess and the Abode of Love.

FOURTEEN
GROUND STRAFER

Between May 18th and November 19th I had taken part in forty-five combats, some with two-seaters, some with fighters, and although in dog-fights with Albatroses my machine had several times been riddled with bullets, I had never once been shot down. This was largely because I was lucky enough to be led by a doughty and clever flight-commander, Captain Scott, with the result that apart from one pilot killed in a flying accident, of all my companions in these forty-five combats, only one had been lost through enemy action. The other two flights of 46 Squadron were not so fortunate, for in the same period they met with twenty casualties.

During the eleven days between November 20th and 30th, when I took part in low-flying work in the Battle of Cambrai, I was engaged on only seven ground-attack sorties, but on three of them I was shot down from the ground, each time narrowly escaping with my life and my liberty. On one of these trips my companion pilot was killed, on another my number two became prisoner of war. The squadron in this period suffered seven casualties, of which four were in my flight.

These figures are evidence of how very dangerous ground-strafing could be compared with routine air fighting, even though we flew obsolescent Pups against high-performance Albatroses. My own experience was but typical, for a thirty per cent casualty rate was averaged each day of active operations by the four fighter squadrons allocated to low flying attacks in this brief but exciting offensive.

What happened to me in the eleven days, which were more packed with thrills and nerve-racking moments than any other comparable spell in my time in France, has been described lengthily enough in my book *No Parachute*, in accounts which were written at the time. Here in this chapter I will do no more than recall some of the highlights that have stayed strongest in my memory.

Undoubtedly one incident that I still recall with disquiet was when my fuel tank was hit while I was flying at 300 feet, and I looked over my tail to see petrol pouring out and vaporising in the heat of the engines' exhaust. This was the one time in my active service flying when I really panicked with fear—the fear of the plane bursting into flames, and of my being burnt alive. I had but one thought, to get down to earth, and that I did within seconds.

The first time I was shot down, my Camel was caught in the burst of a shell close to the ground, and I dropped with disrupted controls on to a convenient stretch of level ground, which owing to the fluidity of the ground fighting I did not realise lay between our forward troops, occupying hastily dug trenches below Cantaing, and the line of German outposts along La Folie Wood opposite. I was indeed lucky to escape, but the Camel remained in no-man's-land.

On my third forced descent, I was hit by archie over the Bourlon area, where in a fierce struggle below, our foremost troops were advancing in the morning and retreating in the afternoon, so that I did not know until I touched down whether or not I was a prisoner. Another anxious moment to remember!

There were other happenings that remained in the memory without any effort. One was when, on the first morning of the attack, soon after dawn, with clouds almost to the ground, 'C' Flight passed at twenty feet over the tanks advancing across the Hindenburg Line. We were on our way to bomb batteries at Lateau Wood, and the vision of those then new-fangled monsters rolling forward in smoke and mist, with supporting infantry casually strolling a few paces behind each one, was something quite unforgettable.[1]

Another highlight spectacle was the line of burnt-out tanks that were caught at point-blank range on the ridge at Flesquières, a check that unhinged the whole offensive. Another was a glimpse of one of my bombs bursting with deadly effect in the centre of a crowd of German support troops waiting well behind the lines. Yet another, soon afterwards, was of a second bomb falling among a smaller group, when as I steeply banked, I saw the burst sending them flying into the air, one man with his arms and legs outstretched like a letter X, his rifle still grasped in a lifeless hand.

Compared with such grisly moments, two other abiding incidents were almost commonplace. One was when having landed in the mist to discover my position, and seeing what I thought was a troop of our cavalry galloping across the field towards me, I found they were Germans. I had come down on the wrong side of the Lines! The second happened during a dive attack on a nest of machine-guns, when, above the roar of the engine and the rattle of my guns, I heard an extraordinary noise, a loud twang. I had no idea what it was until, on the way home, I noticed the two ends of one of my flying wires flapping loose. It had been severed by a bullet, but fortunately the duplicated wire held.

My experiences were in no way out of the ordinary, for almost every pilot could tell of narrow escapes. A fellow pilot of 46 Squadron managed to fly into a metal chimney while attacking troops sheltering in a workshop, and brought back a length of piping attached to his wing. A flight commander in 64 Squadron, our neighbours at Izel le Hameau, was shot down in a D.H.5 in open ground, came at once under fire, took refuge in an advancing tank, and from then on enjoyed the experience of taking part in a tank attack. Another D.H.5. pilot of 68 Squadron, hit by a shell while attacking troops near Bourlon Wood, and forced to come down ahead of our infantry, saw a 64

---

[1]An extract from my account of this episode, written years later at the R.A.F. Staff College, is quoted in the *Official History of the War—The War in the Air*, by H. A. Jones, Vol IV, pp. 236–7.

Squadron D.H.5. crash nearby which had just been shot down by Richtofen. He ran across under fire, helped the trapped pilot to free himself, and the two of them managed to make their way back to the British positions.

Another pilot, an Australian of 68 Squadron, spotted three tanks held up in Bourlon Wood by two anti-aircraft guns mounted on lorries and being used as anti-tank guns. These he silenced, and the tanks were able to advance. This was exactly the kind of opportunity target that we were constantly on the look-out for during the early stages of the advance, but that most of us could never find.

A lighter touch was provided by another pilot of 64 Squadron, a high-spirited youngster, who dropped his bombs on a cluster of machine-guns, turned at once, and as he passed over the hamstrung gunners below, raised a hand and greeted them with a rude and derisive gesture. At that instant came a bullet with a mission, for it neatly sliced off one of the mocking fingers.

All these were but minor incidents when seen against the overall assistance which the four low-flying squadrons provided in the attack and the subsequent counter-attack, and because of it, the Army Command were satisfied that ground-strafing fighters had earned the standing of yet another arm to help them win battles. This was a discovery that had developed only during the previous six months.

The employment of aircraft to attack military targets on the ground was invented not by airmen but by the military mind, which having started the war by regarding the aeroplane as an extension of the cavalry, for reconnaissance, welcomed it now as an extension of the artillery. The first experiments, made early in May, towards the end of the Battle of Arras, were carried out by F.E.2bs of 12 Squadron and Nieuports of 60 Squadron in direct support of a Third Army attack along the Scarpe Valley, and their efforts were so much approved that in the brief Battle of Messines in early June, fourteen pilots drawn from six fighter squadrons went out on roving missions to attack enemy troops behind the battle area. These also proved so rewarding that similar missions were undertaken sporadically, mostly by single-seater fighters, throughout the Third Battle of Ypres. This was when the pattern of the intensive use of fighters for trench straf-ing, as also for shooting up troops in rear areas, and bombing more distant targets such as aerodromes, became established.

The Battle of Cambrai provided the chance for a really major ef-fort in low-flying work, when two squadrons of Camels and two of D.H.5s were allotted to attack artillery positions and aerodromes in planned support of the surprise breakthrough by tanks. The low clouds and mist did not stop this co-operation but prevented the ac-curate results which were expected had the weather been fine. But inevitably, with clouds down to 100 feet and heavy mist below, some pilots could not find their targets, and those that did were too occu-pied with not crashing into each other or into the ground to con-centrate on meticulous bombing.

For the rest of the Cambrai operation, the pilots of the four squadrons went out two, three or four times a day to bomb and shoot, sometimes on selected objects, such as emplaced batteries, but mostly on opportunity targets in the forward battle area, which usu-ally meant temporarily entrenched infantry or field batteries. As an alternative, some pilots went over the forward troops, whose positions changed from hour to hour, and shot up targets in rear.

The four special squadrons were 3 and 46, newly equipped with Camels, and 64 and the Australian 68, equipped with the D.H.5. The Camels were rightly regarded by higher authority as much better for ground-strafing than heavy-engined planes such as S.E.5a's and Spads, which could not be pulled out of a steep, low dive so readily as a Camel. The D.H.5 was favoured for low work because it was of little use for anything else.

Prior to the opening of the battle, all four squadrons had been al-lowed a couple of weeks' practice in low cross-country flying, oth-erwise contour-chasing, otherwise hedge-hopping, the very crime for which, a few weeks earlier, we could have been court-martialled. The one difficulty we found during these trips at fifty feet was that as the Camel was surprisingly tail heavy, continuous pressure was needed on the joystick to hold her level. At a reasonable height there was room for slight up and down movements, but near the ground, because she was so sharply sensitive, for and aft as well as laterally, there was no margin for error, and one could not relax for a second.

Nevertheless, we quickly accustomed ourselves to this foible, and finding that we became quite expert in our bomb-dropping practices on the aerodrome, rather looked forward in our innocence to having a good time shooting up German staff cars and similar soft-shell targets well behind the enemy lines. It was perhaps fortunate that we had no conception of what really lay ahead.

That our attacks on the 20th were made in the worst possible weather, although productive of casualties and missed targets, did afterwards appear as a blessing in disguise, for we realised that it gave us the benefit of complete surprise, an advantage which vanished in the clearer weather of later operations. The result was that while the earlier casualties were due mostly to pilots flying into trees and other obstacles, later casualties were caused by fire from the ground.

Apart from the matter of risk, there were several major difficulties over effectively attacking pinpoint targets in the forward area, especially with the 20 lb bomb. In thick weather, you had little chance of doing calm and careful aiming, which was carried out by diving the machine at the target and releasing the bomb at the right moment. If too high, you'd certainly miss, if too low, your machine might be hit by fragments of the exploding bomb, or even of the target. If the enemy were already firing at you, you tended to release the bombs much too high, and yet anything short of a direct hit was a waste of effort.

Batteries of artillery were favourite targets for staff officers to pinpoint for us, and when in action were easily found by the gun-flash, but they were hard to put out of action with small bombs, as the gun itself was undamaged by anything but an unlikely hit on the breech. The best answer for field guns was to kill off the crews with bullets. Better still, batteries in known emplacements should have been dealt with, and much more effectively than by 20 lb bombs, by our own artillery.

Machine-guns were even more tricky than artillery because they were difficult to find, and while you were anxiously circling round at 100 feet searching for them, they could be aiming in comfort at you—as I found to my cost at Bourlon Wood. To dive into a nest of machine-guns already firing at you was of course the surest way to bring your war to an instant conclusion.

An occasional predicament with bombs, which were attached to racks under the fuselage, was that they sometimes refused to drop off when you pulled the toggle. You then had the risk of meeting a Hun aeroplane and being unable to get rid of your load to fight him, or of later landing with the near certainty of the bombs being shaken off and detonating under you.

A positive disadvantage of attacking troops with your guns was that with only 700 or so rounds to expend, you could use the whole supply in under a minute's continuous firing, and had then to return to the aerodrome to re-load. To attack a target in short bursts meant repeated dives and repeated risks—increased risks also if on the same target, for the troops would be alerted. Unless you disposed of at least twenty or thirty of the enemy, you were wasting your time, and when the target was entrenched troops, you would be lucky to hit half a dozen, as they could always take cover when they saw you coming.

But the greatest disadvantage of trench-strafing was the danger to oneself and one's plane, especially when diving really low. A good machine-gunner could score a hit at 2,000 feet, and at 300 feet an aeroplane diving straight into his barrels was a gift. When there was one machine-gun, there were always others near, as well as scores, or hundreds of rifles. You did not need to make many dives on such targets to run out of luck.

Over and above all these inflictions, was the painful disadvantage that while you were searching for your target, you were liable to be jumped by bombless fighters diving down from on high, when you, with bombs still on, and neglecting your tail for your target, were likely to be despatched with ease.

There was of course a vital distinction between trench-strafing and ground-strafing, which meant attacking troops behind the lines. In trench attacks the odds were all against you, the possible gains slight. But to shoot up targets in rear, such as marching infantry or transport on roads, or concentrations of waiting reserves, or aerodrome hangars and aeroplanes on the ground, was not only productive of worthwhile results, but was reasonably safe—and could even be exhilarating!

Without exception, every fighter pilot heartily abominated trench-strafing, not only because of poor results for much jeopardy, but because blind chance played too big a part. The fighter pilot and to a lesser degree, other flyers, once they had gained some experience of air fighting, always had the feeling that in their duelling combats, even when flying inferior performance machines, their lives depended on their skill, wits, boldness and accurate shooting. Moreover, if you were the victor, everyone knew of it, and you received proper credit.

But in trench-strafing, you were not fighting, but just attacking well-protected men in trenches, with scores of weapons firing at you, and at you only. Any bullet could hit you, and there was nothing you could do to avoid it. Skill, experience, boldness, none of these counted, everything was sheer chance. Nobody in the R.F.C. knew whether you had done any real damage, and even if you had it did not count as a victory, in fact it counted for nothing. The only way you could show that you'd even been in action was to be shot down or to return with your machine well peppered with bullet-holes.

Having to engage in these dangerous and thankless duties, which we never ceased to dislike intensely, made us feel in a similar condition of indiscriminate carnage as the infantry. The man in the trenches was the creature of fate, with no scope to evade danger by swift action or trained judgement or even sheer flight, but obeying orders without question while death and injury blindly smote him. This was the antithesis of air fighting, where your life lay in your own hands, where you used every trick you knew both to avoid your opponent's bullets and to put bullets into him. More, if you were outclassed, you could always, if you were able, quite honourably make a run for it!

An important factor in our antipathy to trench-strafing was the intense nervous strain. Unless you were made of steel and completely impervious to fear, you had to summon all your will-power to dive into a nest of guns, with hundreds of carefully aimed bullets coming up at you. Your brain and your senses were numbed, your spirit shrank from so inevitable and futile an end, for it would be a miracle if you weren't hit, and you couldn't rely on miracles indefinitely.

To me, and to every fighter pilot with whom I discussed this subject, then and later in 1918, low-flying attacks were, with few exceptions, a wasteful employment of highly trained pilots and expensive aeroplanes. A 30 per cent rate of casualties meant a new squadron every fourth day and one rendered useless for normal air fighting duties. This situation developed in 46 Squadron when after a week's losses, all but a handful of our pilots were straight out from England, and several routine patrols had to be carried out by the three surviving flight commanders, of whom I was one.

Setbacks such as these could be justified only if positive and valuable results were obtained, and in the Cambrai offensive these were not frequent. It is true that behind the lines, roving fighters did play havoc against troops such as reinforcements on the march, but even these successes did not greatly affect the course of the battle, if at all. They had nuisance value only. As for resolute and experienced troops in deep trenches, they mostly regarded low-flying attacks as just another pest, like snipers, trench-mortars and rainstorms.

Certainly much more notable results could have been obtained in both the attack and the German counter-attack had the overall plan for the operation included a system for tank crews as well as infantry to call on aircraft for help in emergency by some distinctive rocket signal. I met none of this in the ground fighting until the German break-through on November 30th, when, as I saw from the air, Very lights went up by the score, but they signified only a general emergency, and indicated no specific targets for us to investigate.

Perhaps the most cogent reason advanced by the Army in favour of low-flying attacks was that they stimulated the morale of troops in action. Unquestionably the Army knew best, but as an airman experienced in being shot down among infantry, I took this theory with a grain of salt. Unless the co-operating fighter flew directly over the heads of the infantry, and attacked objectives within their vision, they were just not aware of what assistance was being given.

I had this brought home to me when I came down near Bourlon Wood, where fighters had co-operated very usefully with tanks in the earlier stages of the attacks in this difficult objective. In conversation with a group of infantry officers, I mentioned that my squadron had taken an active part in this fighting, and received the answer, 'Oh, were our planes up?'

When General Trenchard visited 46 Squadron on November 25th to praise our work in the offensive I mentioned this incident to his A.D.C., Maurice Baring, who was very perceptive to its point.[1] He also agreed when I told him how the infantry on the one hand credited us with an unwarranted capacity for astonishing achievement, and on the other could not understand why we failed to do things that to them were perfectly simple.

An example of the former occurred when I was caught by a shell burst south of Cantaing and came down with my controls gone in a large field which was in fact no-man's-land. The captain of the 9th Royal Scots whose trenches I eventually reached, thought I had landed deliberately to bring him information about the fighting in Fontaine, where I had been shooting up German reinforcements coming from Cambrai. He expected that I would then return to the Camel, start it, and take off, all under machine-gun fire from La Folie Wood. He was more than surprised when I said I was walking home.

As for the second misconception, the infantry expected us, flying at 100 miles an hour, to see unremarkable things below, such as a well-hidden machine-gun holding up a section of the advance, or a battery such as caused the check at Flesquières. But it was a matter of luck to spot such situations, indeed while flying around Fontaine and Cantaing, I had not even noticed the Royal Scots' trenches, nor the Germans in La Folie Wood. When we did see and could intervene, then we might do something really useful, as the 68 Squadron pilot did with the anti-tank guns.

[1] He quoted the conversation in his book *R.F.C., H.Q., 1914–18,* pp. 260–1.

In spite of these various misapprehensions, when the infantry realised that we had tried to help them, they were always generously forthcoming in expressing their appreciation. The classic example of this response occurred when an enemy strong-point held up the advance on Bourlon Wood on November 23rd, and a pilot of 68 Squadron, Lieutenant A. Griggs, of American birth, noticing the hold-up, made repeated dives on the German position until at last he was killed. A year later the *In Memoriam* column of *The Times* contained this entry: 'To an UNKNOWN AIRMAN, shot down 23rd November, 1917, whilst attacking a German strong-point south-west of Bourlon Wood, in the effort to help out a Company of the Royal Irish Rifles, when other help had failed.'[1]

Such incidents, valiant as they were, and unquestionably inspiring to the infantry, could only confirm the unenthusiastic views of most fighter pilots on the undue risk and wastage of low-flying attacks, especially in the forward lines. But these views were not shared by Higher Authority, which the work of fighters in the Cambrai offensive confirmed in the opinion, held also by the German High Command, that low-flying attacks were a powerful weapon in battle. They may have been right, but those of us who had to do the dirty work still held to the conviction that ground-strafing, and especially trench-strafing, was a very expensive luxury. As for me, I had come to the conclusion well before the end of the Cambrai interlude that rather than face a single trench-strafing foray, I would much prefer to go through half a dozen dog-fights with Albatroses.

[1] Quoted from *The War in the Air*, by H. A. Jones, Vol. IV., p. 246.

FIFTEEN

THE RED BARON

When I joined No. 46 Squadron in May, the repute of Baron Manfred von Richtofen was already so high that he had not only become a symbol of the superiority of German fighter aeroplanes and their pilots, but had taken on the standing of a super-slayer, dominating the air fighting on the British Front, and invariably present in any combat involving Albatros fighters.

The only other German fighter pilots whose names were equally familiar to the Royal Flying Corps were Immelmann and Boelcke, who were both dead, and Voss, and these, with Richtofen, had won renown comparable with that of the French aces, Guynemer and Nungesser. The only British pilot whose name was widely known was Ball, and then only after he was killed.

Through British newspaper reports taken from German Air Service communiqués we knew that Richtofen was piling up his list of victories over British aeroplanes with a speed that was appalling, though those who were flying against him knew that he found his victims largely among our obsolete and inefficient two-seaters. This was seen during the Battle of Arras, when in the one ill-fated month of April—Bloody April—the twenty-one planes that he destroyed included seven defenceless B.E.s and five decrepit F.E.2b and 2d pushers.

His score in this battle would have reached a much higher figure had he not gone on leave on May 1st with fifty-two victories to his credit. By the second half of May the centre of air activity had moved to the Ypres front, as a preliminary to the Battle of Messines, and here 46 Squadron frequently encountered the Red Baron's Jasta 11, which, though then stationed near Douai, east of Arras, flew daily to the busier northern sector.

The quality of the Albatros formations that we met varied considerably, some so lacking aggressiveness, even against our inferior performance Pups, that we concluded they consisted of fighter pilot pupils from a *Jastaschule*, possibly the one at Valenciennes. But the majority were ably and boldly led, and among them the red-patterned D–IIIs of Richtofen's Jasta were outstanding. Because during his absence on leave this group behaved with its customary vigour we did not for a moment realise that the Red Baron was not among our opponents, and that his unit was being led by his brother, Lothar. Not until a month or so afterwards did we discover this through the German communiqués.

Most of our fights with the Circus, as Richtofen's Jasta had become familiarly known, partly because of the showy colourings, always including red, of its machines, were inconclusive, for though his hand-picked pilots were mounted on better aeroplanes, the Pup was too nimble at height for them to bring accurate fire to bear during a swift, hectic dog-fight. On the other hand, the Pup, with its lower speed, could seldom achieve a position to deliver a lethal burst with its single gun. But we did manage to stay alive!

My very first dog-fight on May 31st, in which my patrol was attacked at 16,000 feet, was with Jasta 11, but the whole affair was so sudden and confusing that I retained no coherent recollection of what happened, other than of wildly skidding clear of shots from behind me and firing short bursts at a red and green machine and then at a yellow and red, both of which suddenly appeared in my sights. Fortunately for us, the fight ended quickly, as three Sopwith Triplanes intervened and the Huns withdrew, for me just in time, for my gun had jammed. But one of the enemy was able to put a group of bullets through the fuselage just behind me, as I found when I landed.

My second encounter with Albatroses occurred a couple of days later when another pilot and I fell into an ambush while attacking a two-seater. Six D–IIIs dived on us, and, though my companion drew clear, I was trapped, and they followed me down from 12,000 feet to 500, taking shots at me in turn. Miraculously I escaped being hit, nor was my machine vitally damaged. The only clue I had to my attackers' identity was the yellow spinner on the propeller of the first Hun to open fire close behind me, and from then on I was diving vertically with full engine, with bullets cracking round my head, and much too petrified to think even of glancing back momentarily. My companion thought he saw the tell-tale red of the Circus, but I felt that had he been correct the shooting would have been much more accurate.

Yet another encounter with what we presumed to be the Circus came on June 4th, when once more we were attacked, but this time at 18,000 feet. In a confused scramble, I again had a red and green machine in my sights, and gave him a brief burst, but he dived clear. At this height the Pups had the tactical advantage, and one of the enemy was shot down, to crash near Roulers.

On June 5th, a patrol of nine, for which I was reserve but was not called upon, had a succession of brushes with the Circus, two and possibly three of which were driven down with no loss, though our machines were badly mauled. Prior to meeting the Pups the Circus had attacked a formation of Sopwith 1½-strutters of 45 Squadron, of which two were destroyed, one shot down on enemy territory, and two forced to crash in the British Lines. The two-seaters were hopelesssly out-classed by the D–IIIs, and even the Pups, fighting at 12,000 feet, were fortunate to escape a similar disaster.

During the three weeks that followed, although I took part in a few fights with Albatroses, in one of which we claimed a flamer, they were not of the Circus. Afterwards I learned that one group could have been Jasta 7, for they attacked us from below, the machines hanging on their propellers, and this was a tactical method favoured by this unit's commander, Joseph Jacobs.

But on June 29th six of us were dived on by eight Albatroses, again at 18,000 feet, and of these about half carried the red markings of

Richtofen's Jasta. Once more a brief, exciting dog-fight followed, and again a couple of our opponents dropped out, but we could not see whether they were damaged or even hit. The fight ended as before with the lightly loaded Pups in possession.

Back at the aerodrome we assumed that some of Richtofen's Jasta had been joined by pilots from another unit, and much later we learned that we were probably right, for on the 26th June Richtofen, who had returned from leave on the 14th, had formed Jagdgeschwader No. 1, a group of four units comprising his own Jasta 11 and numbers 4, 6 and 10. This was the Circus proper, J.G.1, designed and equipped for mobility, and able to move quickly along the front wherever urgently needed.

By this time the prestige attaching to Richtofen's name had become a significant factor in the morale of the R.F.C. To every young airman arriving at the squadron he was an accepted bogey, epitomising all the dangers that faced a newcomer. His all-pervading presence kept his name constantly on our lips in the Mess, for even seasoned pilots were not immune from the menace that his existence posed. To encounter a formation of Albatroses created no alarm, for they might well be a group of indifferently led and mostly inexperienced pilots, wary even of Pups, but if we spotted the flash of red paint we knew we must nerve ourselves to an almost inevitably lethal fight, with the odds loaded against us. And if fighter pilots had this complex, how much more intimidating must have been the threat of the Red Baron to the occupants of third grade two-seaters, whose only hope was to flee before he came within shooting distance.

Yet Richtofen was no superman, and by no means a super-pilot. He was brave but he was wary, seldom entering into a free-for-all dog-fight, where chance played as important a role as skill, but waiting on the fringe for stragglers. Then he would pounce. When he did take part in close in-fighting, he usually had wing-men to protect his tail. But the acknowledged ascendancy he had acquired, so cleverly exploited by the German propaganda organisation, gave him an immeasurable prestige, which even then was becoming a mystique, and yet he was worthy of it, for he was a natural fighter and leader and a stranger to fear, at least until he was wounded.

At the beginning of July, 46 Squadron moved south from La Gorgue to Bruay, and from here we operated on standby duties with No 8 Naval Squadron at Mont St Eloi, to the west of the Vimy Ridge. There had been ferocious fighting on this front during the Battle of Arras, both on the ground and in the air, but now the sector was quiet, and Richtofen's units sought their prey further north.

On July 6th, while chasing an enemy two-seater over the Scarpe Valley, Courtneidge and I saw a fight in progress to our flank, and turned at once to join in. Four F.E.s had resorted to their usual tactical merry-go-round in defence against the attacks of four D–IIIs, but these, as we drew near and opened fire, withdrew east. At about the same time, some thirty miles to the north, six other F.E.2d's had also adopted the defensive circle to resist the attacks of Jasta 11, led by Richtofen, which was joined by other Albatroses until some forty German fighters were engaged. The F.E.s, reinforced now by four Triplanes of 10 Naval Squadron, fought with their customary stubbornness, and although two of them were destroyed, they and the Triplanes sent down several Huns.

The pilot of one of these was Richtofen, wounded in the head by a long-range shot by an F.E. observer. Lucky to get away with his life, the Red Baron managed to crash-land near Wervicq before losing consciousness. After that lesson he knew that even he might one day fail to be the victor. Other pilots, both German and British, could well have rested on their laurels after so narrow an escape, and devoted their energies to administration or staff work in the higher echelons of the Air Service, but not Richtofen, and though he knew that any fight might be his last, as it might for all of us, his courage and resolution never faltered.

We saw no more of Richtofen or of the Circus for several weeks, for 46 Squadron was called to England to fend off day-bombing Gothas, whose attacks on London had infuriated and alarmed both people and government. Not until the end of August did we return to France, to plunge at once into the savage fighting, again both on the ground and in the air, of the Third Battle of Ypres. By this time

Richtofen was back in the cockpit, and from September 2nd onwards was flying a new fighter, the Fokker Triplane, his first victim being an R.E.8 on September 2nd.

46's opening patrol of five on the morning of September 3rd was made by 'A' Flight, which as it moved eastwards towards Menin was attacked by Richtofen and five members of Jasta 11. The Pup pilots, full of confidence but out of combat practice for seven weeks, and matched now against the D–V as well as the Triplane, were over-whelmed. Two were shot down in enemy territory, one to die of wounds, the other, Richtofen's opponent, to be a prisoner. A third pilot managed to reach the British Lines, the two others limped home riddled with bullets.

The second patrol, by 'B' Flight, suffered a similar fate when it met Jasta 4 of J.G.1. One pilot was shot down and made prisoner, another was wounded but reached our Lines, and the others were severely shot up, though this time one of the enemy was sent down out of control.

Next came the turn of 'C' Flight, and our approach to the air bat-tle at 14,000 feet, knowing full well what to expect, was a sight that has always stayed in the memory, for ahead of us over fifty aeroplanes, dark specks against the clear sky, foe indistinguishable from friend, were swirling in a vast cloud, turning, diving, zooming, fighting, with here and there a speck falling vertically, two of them in flames. We rode into the middle of it, anticipating a furious fight within seconds, but for at least five minutes clashed with no enemy formation. Then Scott, our leader, dived intrepidly on seven D–Vs that appeared just below us. In this fracas we would have been no less roughly handled than 'A' and 'B' Flights, for we were at the same disadvantage of height, but luckily a formation of Camels roared up and took over the fight. These Huns had no red paint and were not of Jasta 11, but afterwards we concluded that judged by their boldness and skill they were one of the units of J.G.1.

Next day a 'C' Flight patrol in which I did not take part was at-tacked from the rear by Richtofen in the Triplane, attended by only one henchman of Jasta 11. He did not stay when he saw that his presence was discovered. The same day, during a second 'C' Flight patrol of eight, we engaged four Jasta 11 pilots, all with their badge of red, and were beginning a brisk little dog-fight when no fewer than fourteen more Albatroses dived down from on high to join in. Fortunately there were so many of them all trying to secure favourable firing positions that they got in each other's way, and exploiting our manœuvrability to the utmost we all fantastically escaped, and though every machine was hit several times, not one pilot was touched.

On September 6th, while on patrol in the early morning, I at last encountered the Fokker, painted all red, and therefore in the deadly hands of Richtofen. We were a two-flight formation of ten and the Triplane was backed by eight D–Vs, but strangely no dog-fight developed, for no leader in either group would initiate an attack. At last the Triplane, using its impressive climb, rose above the others and made a series of dive and zoom attacks on outriders of our two flights. I happened to be one of the pilots he selected to attack, and he hit my Pup's starboard upper wing, as I found when I returned to the aerodrome at St Marie Cappelle. As I heard his bullets I banked sharply and fired a short burst towards him, and the tracer seemed to be on the target, but he zoomed up and drew back to the cover of his formation.

I was highly elated to have exchanged shots with the Red Baron and still be around, and only years later was I to learn that he went on convalescent leave this very day, though he might still have put in that early-morning flight in the hope of winning one more victory. The net result of this encounter, which should have evolved into a signal battle, was that the Triplane went off, eastwards, and the rest followed him.

Following on this inconclusive skirmish, 46 moved south to the Arras area, and here for two and a half months we saw nothing of the Circus, which was fully occupied in the fighting for Passchendaele. We did not then know it, but since August 17th, a second Circus had existed, J.G.2, formed of Jastas 12, 13, 15 and 19, and based opposite our new front, but although we met its several units many times, we never had the feeling that we were up against very seasoned pilots, as usually occurred when opposed to Richtofen's command.

Not until the Cambrai offensive did he come again into 46 Squadron's orbit. The dramatic penetration of the Hindenburg Line by tanks on November 20th created a critical situation for the German High Command, and on November 22nd, J.G.1 was moved hastily south, the first patrols being made that same day. The news of Richtofen's arrival spread among us immediately.

The pilots of 46 were now mounted on Camels, and those of us who had fought for months at a great disadvantage on Pups would have welcomed an opportunity to tilt a lance with the red D–Vs and the Fokkers, but it was our fate to be employed on the dangerous and unpopular work of ground-strafing, On several occasions when we could have found fights, we were carrying bombs, and with their weight even the Camel could not enter into air combat.

Only when the bombs had been dropped could we, ignoring our orders to complete our sortie by firing at ground troops, rise above to seek an Albatros. Some of our pilots did destroy J.G.1 aircraft, but for my part, I never learned whether the D–V which I shot down between Moeuvres and Bourlon Wood on November 30th, after a low-bombing attack, was from Jasta 11 or not, for I sighted it so unexpectedly, attacked so instantaneously, then banked so violently to avoid a collision as it fell, that I never had the chance to check the colourings. Even if not Jasta 11, the plane could have come from Jasta 10, for my companion on this patrol, Lieutenant R. E. Dusgate, who was shot down in this same area, was, as I long afterwards learned, claimed by one of the pilots of this unit of J.G.1.

This was my last even possible encounter with a member of Richtofen's Circus, and I was not sorry. Indeed, I was relieved to be alive, for when the word passed round the R.F.C. squadrons engaged in the Cambrai attack that the Bad Baron, as we sometimes called him, had joined our party, we all knew that there were nasty days ahead, in spite of our Camels and S.E.5a's. In the event, Richtofen himself shot down only two machines during his spell at Cambrai, a D.H.5 over Bourlon Wood on November 23rd, and an S.E.5a over Moeuvres on November 30th. Thus although I did not meet him, he could have been somewhere near when I sent down the D–V in the same area and perhaps about the same time as he sent down the S.E.

Looking back over these several clashes with Richtofen's Jasta 11 and later with his full Circus, I realise how much the simple fact that he and his pilots were on one's front and could be that day's opponents, and that on a Pup one wouldn't stand much of a chance, was positively an influence operating against high morale. Not only did his unique prestige infiltrate the whole of the R.F.C., but astonishingly it also reached our troops in the trenches, who whenever they saw a British aeroplane fall down with broken wings or in flames invariably gave the credit to the ubiquitous Red Devil. Even to them he was a fabled figure, evidence of German air superiority, as no doubt he was with much greater force to the German forward troops. Not without reason did Field Marshal Ludendorff declare that to the German Army Richtofen was worth two divisions. His fame and the pride in his prowess not only stiffened the spirit of all the German fighting forces but uplifted the whole nation.

The German propaganda machine, in deliberately setting out to build up Richtofen as a national hero, as they had done with Immelmann and Boelcke and were currently attempting on a secondary level with Werner Voss and Lothar Richtofen and one or two other top-scoring fighter pilots, were following the example set by the French whose leading aces were an inspiration to all their fighting men as well as to the non-combatant civilians. Accounts of the glorious feats of both German and French aces received world-wide publicity, especially in the United States, where the absence of similar reports on the work of British flyers sometimes caused raised eyebrows.

The precedent set by the French and Germans was followed by Belgium, Austria, Italy and in due course America. Only the British stubbornly refused to publicise their successful airmen. We in the R.F.C. could not understand this stick-in-the-mud attitude, and did not realise that it was due chiefly to our own much-respected chief, General Trenchard. In the summer of 1917, Field Marshal Haig wrote to the C.I.G.S. in London that he—which meant Trenchard—considered it 'both unwise policy and unfair to other branches of the service to differentiate the treatment of the R.F.C.' and that 'such special treatment would be invidious and likely to cause jealousy both inside and outside the R.F.C.'

That other countries did advertise the exploits of their aces 'would not justify any departure from the well-established customs of the British Army,' declared the Haig–Trenchard memorandum. Yet when Ball was killed and posthumously awarded the Victoria Cross, Trenchard, again through Haig, did not hesitate to write: 'The record of his deeds will stir the pride and admiration of his countrymen, and act as an example and incentive to those who have taken up his work.' One may well reflect that if Ball could become a source of inspiration after he was dead, he could have been a source of perhaps even greater inspiration while he was alive—had his deeds been published fully in the Press.

The day-to-day combats of our fighting airmen were briefly noted in the matter-of-fact R.F.C. communiqué, commonly known as Comic Cuts, but the Press in Britain, although allowed to mention the achievements, could not name the pilots concerned. Only in citations for gallantry awards were names disclosed, but these did not usually appear until six months after the act of gallantry. Canada, Australia and the other Dominions contrived to disregard these stuffy restrictions, and there were other evasions through journalistic interviews with proud relations, until at last, under angry public pressure, the War Office gave grudging permission to the Press to publish articles on such leaders as McCudden, Bishop, Collishaw and a few others, and later, in 1918, when the cloak of secretiveness was lifted, still others such as Mannock and Barker.

But in the meantime the German and French aces had been elevated to a pinnacle of glory and honour such as even our most successful fighters could never afterwards attain, even though their scores of victories were higher than those of their rivals. And more, a score of British stars had blazed across the embattled skies of France whose names were unknown outside the flying services and to half those within.

How many of the general public ever heard of A. W. Beauchamp-Proctor or Don MacLaren, sharing fifth place in the list of British aces, each with fifty-four victories, which would have put them third in the German list and second with Guynemer in the French? Or R. A. Little with forty-seven, only one fewer than the famous Voss, or R. F. Fullard and G. E. H. McElroy, each with forty-six victories, a higher tally than Nungesser, Boelcke or Lothar Richtofen, all of world-wide renown? Or of A. E. Mckeever, the greatest two-seater fighter pilot of the war, twenty-fifth in the British list, with thirty kills, which would have placed him seventh in both French and German lists?

That these men and others of almost equal prowess were, until the later stages of the war, almost as anonymous as civil servants was due entirely to the bovine obstinacy of British service officialdom, whose mistaken concepts were typical of the rigid conservatism of the older military mentality that brought so many grievous troubles on our heads throughout World War I.

What Trenchard and those who thought like him failed to realise was that human beings need heroes, indeed crave for them, especially in wartime. The fighting troops, both in the air and on the ground, need heroes to set the standards, to lead in aggressive action, to excite imitative valour, or as Haig wrote about Ball 'to act as an example and incentive'. The populace at home need heroes to light the way, to sustain courage, to inspire patriotism, or again as was said of Ball, 'to stir the pride and admiration of his countrymen'.

In war there are many heroes, but from all the vast numbers that fought on the ground in France very few could be so outstandingly conspicuous in gallantry as to become nationally famed and honoured. But the airmen were different, for they were a race apart, a new breed of warrior, fighting in single combat in the skies overhead, where all could see them. Those who vanquished their airborne foes and went on vanquishing them were inevitably acclaimed as heroes, and a hero who flew was a hero to the infantry and gunners just as much as to his fellow flyers. Even more could he have been a hero to the people at home, for though his exploits might not be witnessed, they appealed vividly to the imagination, the vision of knightly combat among the clouds.

But our hidebound policies threw away, at least until the last phases of the war, the contribution which the vicarious sharing of heroic deeds by the civilian populace could have made to the national will to stand firm, especially during the black year of 1917, when disaster threatened us at sea and a future of futile massacre on land. The names and achievements of our warriors of the air, the aces whom everybody could salute as heroes, should have been blazoned throughout the Empire, and in America, just as were those of Richtofen and Guynemer and the other earlier aces.

We should have built up our heroes as national assets, as did our enemies and allies. We need never have gone to the extreme of the German authorities in concentrating most of their official lionising on the one outstanding figure of Richtofen, for this course held the important disadvantage, already seen to a lesser degree with Immelmann and Boelcke, that when the hero was killed the whole nation was plunged into despondency. The remedy for this was to build up several heroes at the same time, so that the loss of one of them produced no calamitous gloom.

Another danger that we could have avoided was the German and French encouragement of comparative scoring tables, for these led to competitive head-hunting by the leading aces, to unworthy rivalries, and to the taking of unnecessary risks to obtain another victory.

Yet even in their excessive spot-lighting of Richtofen, the German authorities built better than they knew, for they created a national paladin who in the course of time was to mean as much to the Germanic people as Nelson does to the English. Even during his lifetime, the Red Baron became a legend, and not only to the Germans but to his adversaries, for ruthless as he was, and selfishly dedicated to no higher impulse than head-hunting, he won his opponents' respect and admiration.

Though he had killed so many British airmen, they were mostly slain in fair combat, for it was not his fault that the R.F.C. was for so

183

long equipped with ineffective aeroplanes. The majority of those who fought against him bore him no ill-will, and from my own experience up to the end of 1917 I can say that there was never any element of hatred towards him or any other German flyer. When he was killed, he was given every military honour, and the whole of the R.F.C. in France, at that hour become the new-born Royal Air Force, gave him their final salute as a stout-hearted and worthy adversary.

Typical of the average British fighter pilot's attitude to Richtofen, as to most of the well-known enemy aces—and as we were to learn later, very often of theirs to us—was the comment which I read in the wartime diary of an eighteen-year-old Camel pilot who was wounded on April 6th, 1918. In France his squadron, No. 65, had suffered casualties at the hands of Richtofen's Circus and the Boelcke and other Jastas, yet back in England in hospital he could write on April 23rd: 'Cavalry Captain Baron von Richtofen has met his match and has been shot down and killed. Good work! Rest the soul of a brave man and a fine pilot.'[1]

In his death Richtofen took on the stature of an immortal, and so was born the epic of knightly valour that persisted through the German defeat, was continued when the stricken German people sought some symbol to assuage their wounded pride, and remained unsullied even through the unknightly excesses of the Second World War.

Today in Germany the Richtofen mystique is as strong as ever, and strangely it has blossomed in the United States in a most unexpected way, not only among serious students and historians of the air fighting in World War I, but among tens of thousands of 'buffs' who on a different level are enthusiastically dedicated to their interest in the pilots and aeroplanes of the first air war. Partly through the influence of strip cartoons, especially for the young, the name of the Red Baron is as familiar in the U.S.A. as that of Robin Hood in England. The Red Baron has indeed, with the aid of the frivolous 'Snoopy' comic strips, become practically part of American folklore.

[1] Lieutenant, later Group Captain, Guy M. Knocker.

A bizarre dénouement to the grim events of fifty years before, especially to those who, like me, can well remember the apprehensions his red Albatros and those of his Circus evoked when we met over the battlefields of France, and entered into the fray with little confidence that we would emerge alive.

SIXTEEN
EVENING PATROL

I glanced behind me and saw that the four Camels were gently sliding into their V-formation positions. Well, none had been hit, which was something, but I was very irate at having lost the two Huns, for they had seemed a certainty. I had been leading the patrol for an hour and a half at between 7,000 and 12,000, for it was too cold to go any higher, and had seen no enemy planes at all, when suddenly I spotted the two L.V.G.s.

The snow that had fallen a few days earlier still covered the countryside and made it difficult to recognise familiar landmarks inside enemy territory, though the Lines themselves stood out more distinctly than under normal conditions, for every zigzagging trench was inscribed in black on the white background. Over Hunland I relied chiefly on the straight black lines that were the main high roads and on the smoky masses of the towns.

We were four or five miles over, at 7,000 feet, when I picked up the two dark specks moving slowly westwards across the snowy ground, some three or 4,000 feet below us, and though I couldn't identify them as Huns it was worth going down to make sure. They were to the west of us, and rocking my wings, I dropped into a forty-five-degree dive. After descending 2,000 feet, I saw that they were L.V.G.s and steepened the dive until we were swooping down at 150 miles an hour, with the Camel seeming to like it.

186

The four pilots behind me, Robinson, Edelston, Lambourn and Muir, who were all in my flight, had been told exactly what to do. I'd long ago given up attacking two-seaters from directly astern and above, and my tactics were to go down well behind the Hun, then under the impetus of the dive come up beneath him and fire on a steep climb. Because we were approaching from the east, the observers weren't looking our way, which meant that with any luck we should surprise and get both of them. But I was counting my chickens too soon. When we were still three hundred yards from them I saw and heard tracer flash down towards the left-hand Hun, a dappled black and yellow. I could hardly believe my eyes, for the whole essence of the attack was to withhold fire until we were under them.

It was Lambourn, out on my left, firing a short burst, about fifty rounds, but enough to lose us surprise. There was nothing I could do but to continue the dive, though both the L.V.G.s were already swerving violently while their observers fired wildly at us. Before they could dive we plummeted behind them and came up underneath, and though out of the corner of my eye I saw my companions' tracer smoking up in criss-cross patterns, they didn't seem to be hitting anything. Nor was I, for although I put in a snap burst at the second Hun, painted patch-work green and brown, I was too busy avoiding collision with my enthusiastic followers to be able to think of calm and careful aiming.

The two Huns had by now dipped into a dive, and I half-rolled the Camel into a steep plunge after them, opening fire at 200 yards on the green and brown. By the tracer spurting past me, I knew that the others were close behind, and I could only hope that they'd pulled away to a flank, or else their bullets might too easily come into my back. I continued firing in brief bursts until after about a hundred rounds, one of my Vickers jammed, and the other gun began firing so erratically I feared I'd shoot off my propeller.

Meanwhile the green and brown observer had a clear bead on me, and his tracer was coming so close that I had to swerve aside in the dive as I grabbed the hammer and slammed the cocking handle. The others flashed past, but were soon left behind, for the L.V.G.s were now diving vertically with full engine.

I rectified the jam, but it was too late, the enemy were out of sight. The four Camels were climbing up to rejoin me. Five of us, we must surely have hit the Huns, I thought, yet they'd gone down under good control, observers still firing, and we could claim nothing. That was why I was irate with Lambourn for firing too soon, and as we assembled to continue the patrol, I vowed I'd tear him off a strip when we landed.

We had still another twenty minutes' patrol to do, and steadily climbing, I led the way south, still about five miles over, until we were over Bourlon Wood, where six weeks ago we had been among the flocks of aeroplanes, including Richtofen's Circus, contesting the air above the intense fighting of the Cambrai offensive. But now there was not a single other plane to be seen. Still on the climb, I circled south of Cambrai, then turned north-west for Izel.

Still fuming about the missed Huns, I decided to give Lambourn a real rocket, for he knew well that he hadn't to open fire until he saw my tracer, but then as we flew along, I reflected that after all he was pretty new, he'd only been with us a fortnight, and this was his fourth or fifth patrol, perhaps he was a little too keen, or had become over-excited. And it wasn't so long ago that I was a fledgling myself, and might have done exactly the same, and maybe it was only by chance that I didn't.

Of the other three, Robinson was a fairly practised hand, but two were still novices, though they'd had a couple of weeks longer than Lambourn. They were not so ignorant as I was when I came to 46 in May, a wide-eyed innocent with no idea of what I was in for, and nobody had told me a thing about the snags of air fighting. Because of this experience I tried to teach my chaps something of what I'd learned.

I glanced behind me—one machine was dragging fifty yards in rear. It was Muir. I cursed myself for committing the formation leader's big sin, going too fast for them to keep position. And roaring along on nearly full throttle was, as I well knew, the sure way to produce engine trouble throughout my flight. I reduced speed until he caught up, then kept level at three-quarters throttle.

It was scarcely beyond mid-afternoon, but already the late December day was moving to its close. Above, a steely-blue sky spoke of the coming hard night of winter. Eastwards, I vainly searched the sky for more Huns, and then below, gazing into the snowy whiteness that reached to an horizon already enveloped in hazy gloom. But to the west, the sky was bright and clear, and from our height, 15,000 feet, I looked into the red glow of the wintry sun as it sank towards the rim of the earth. Beneath it, I saw the distant sea, a gleaming streak of red gold, the waters I would before long cross for England.

I throttled back further, and began gradually to descend. The ground below had already lost the sun, and was relapsing into twilight. Ahead of us, stretching across our front, the winding belt of the Lines was revealed by the flicker of occasional gun flashes and shell bursts which in the cold sharp air sparkled like stars. There they were, the P.B.I. and the gunners, starting another evening of bombarding each other, the infantry standing in frosty, snowfilled trenches on guard against other shivering wretches in another set of trenches a hundred yards away. What a hell of a way to wage war, what a mad existence! How fortunate were we, to be up here, gliding down to an aerodrome clear of all this evening hate, where warm quarters and good food awaited us.

I turned to check that all was well with the chaps behind, and wondered whether any of them was thinking the same as me, whether they realised how fortunate they were. Did they feel ever the immensity of what was happening to them and to the millions entrenched below? Did they respond to the magical impact of being nearly three miles up in the sky, and sense as I did when I was a novice eight months ago—and as indeed I sometimes did now when flying high over a vast battle-field—the remoteness, the physical isolation from the normal earthly things below?

Eight months ago! Then I was an initiate, blindly following my patrol leader, tumbling into brief, deadly fights that to me were utter confusion. And now it was I who was the leader, the flight commander giving orders, taking my strings of fledglings into combat—

on this occasion, a combat that had not worked out too well, but still a fight with bullets flying around.

Suddenly, *crump! crump! crump!* just below us, to the right. So archie hadn't packed up yet, in spite of the cold. I applied the slightest touch of right rudder and edged gently towards the bursts, then looked around to make sure my tyros were following, which they were, instinctively, probably not even noticing the minute change of course. But small as it was, it had deceived archie, whose corrected bursts came to our left, where we would have been had we kept straight on. Next another gentle swerve still to the right, again imperceptible from the ground, and once more the bursts came well to the left. Archie had seen through the first swerve and thought my next would return us to my first course, but one never did the expected in this game. Two more bursts, still not near enough to worry us, then he grew tired and gave up. When we reached Izel, I found we had not a single shrapnel-hole.

The Camel's willing Clerget engine, throttle now half closed, purred contentedly as we descended steadily to her home stable. Yes, I thought, I have tried to teach these newcomers something of the trade. I had learned the hard way at the beginning, had to find out things for myself, as also did my fellow fledglings, of whom some were fortunate like me, but others not, and they disappeared. But how quickly we learned, and not only how to fight. I had arrived with scarcely a serious thought in my head, but a few scraps changed all that, in a couple of weeks I had passed into manhood, alive to hazard and to responsibility. All who survived were the same, you could see them maturing after a few dog-fights, still young in years but fledged in prowess.

It had happened to Robinson already, and was now happening to the other three behind me, and to all the other newcomers who had joined the squadron during the last few weeks, fellows like Blakeley, Debenham, Jenkins, MacLaren, Taylor, Falkenburg. Those who had not been through the strain of the Cambrai trench-strafing were tremendously fresh and eager, bursting with impatience to get at the Hun, and no doubt sometimes wondering why I didn't charge bull-headed at every enemy formation we met. But I had survived over half a hundred combats by watching my step, for within days of my arrival I'd learned that my first aim was not to get myself needlessly killed. This had suited me, for I just wasn't one of those hell-bent daredevils like Ball who could dash alone into a crowd of enemies and get away with it by sheer brazen audacity.

'The boldest measures are the safest', said old Nelson, and no doubt he was right, but that was only for the fire-eating minority, and if they were lucky as well as brave they became top aces. Like Thompson, who'd joined 46 Squadron six weeks after me, but who, when we were in scraps together, took risks on Pups that staggered me, and always I was amazed he escaped, but he *did* escape. I realised that each of us fighters was different from the next and that there were various kinds and degrees of courage, but I also knew that my particular brand was to try to stay alive while still getting my Hun.

Thompson was like Ball and didn't care whether he was killed or not, Ferrie was another Thompson, the thought of meeting a grisly end didn't seem to enter his head. Still another was Andrew McK-eever of 11 Squadron at Bellevue—and at this moment, looking down, I saw Bellevue aerodrome over to our left. I'd been there often and talked to him, a normal friendly Canadian, yet here was a man, flying Bristol fighters at a time when they weren't supposed to cross the Lines except in formations of at least six, who on three occasions, while alone except for his rear-gunner, Sergeant Powell, as brave as himself—had attacked Albatros formations of seven, eight and nine, and each time had shot down three or four, and got away almost un-scathed.

But neither McKeever nor any of the other risk-takers could have won through without great luck, for even the bravest, most skilful fighter could be caught by a chance bullet. They were blessed with luck, and nobody in air fighting could get far without it. That ex-plained me, for I too had been lucky. First, I had missed the Battle of Arras by a couple of weeks, the Bloody April of tragic history, and second I had missed most of the Third Battle of Ypres, the ghastly struggle for Passchendaele, when the air fighting reached the most intense level of the year, for with the arrival of our new planes, the German pilots no longer had things their own way. I was glad to avoid the air fighting of these two battles simply because I was flying outdated Pups, but now that I had a Camel and had discovered what a fine machine it was, I knew that had the squadron been equipped with them in May or June, I should not have wanted to miss the Ypres fighting.

As things worked out, I took part in two of the most interesting battles of the war, Messines and Cambrai, both brilliantly conceived and executed, but only brief and minor episodes in the overall business of mass killing—yet both indicating how this war might have been played if the top strategists had not committed themselves and their hapless troops to frontal massacres.

But luck had been with me in other ways. Many times had my machine been riddled with bullets, some passing through my flying clothing, others through my scarf, once under my armpit, yet leaving me untouched except for a graze on the calf. I remembered Armitage, flying close alongside me as we dived on a two-seater whose observer fired at us both, but he was the one who was hit and died. And MacLeod, flying fifty yards behind me at twenty feet in a thick mist, both at great hazard, but it was he who flew into a tree and was killed. And Dusgate, following me on ground-diving attacks over Bourlon, who was hit by archie and became a prisoner, while I was hit by archie and reached our lines. Yes, I had been lucky—perhaps too lucky. I hoped I would not one day have to pay for it.

The patrol was now at 4,000 feet, and the four behind me were there in position as though our planes were tied together. There was still not another aeroplane in the skies. The sun had gone, though the tinge of red lingered above the western horizon, and below us the last of the daylight was slowly surrendering to the coming darkness. We should be back at Le Hameau in good time, but had I gone another ten miles further south of Cambrai, we would have had to land in near darkness.

Looking left, I could still detect Bellevue, and my mind went back to McKeever and to Ball and Thompson and Bishop and all the other fighters without fear. I thought, as I'd done before, how can they do it? What impelled McKeever to plunge into such suicidal risk, against such impossible odds, and three times to perform a deed that should have won him the Victoria Cross?

Because these were acts that I knew I could never have undertaken, I had sometimes asked myself whether I had fully met the challenge of my spell in France. Certainly I had been many times scared, but usually only briefly, in panic situations, such as when the six Albatroses dived on me when I was alone, and again when two practised D–V pilots all but finished me in a dog-fight. What had really shaken me was trench-strafing, but I didn't class this as air fighting. Most of whatever wind-up I'd experienced in combat really came from being mounted on machines which were outranked by the Albatros.

This I knew because of the lift to my morale that piloting a Camel had brought. Now I could meet even a D–V with such wonderful confidence that as soon as I pressed the trigger and saw both guns blazing just in front of me, I felt unbeatable, the scrap was practically over before it started. It was then that I realised with what assurance Richtofen and his crack pilots must have attacked outdated British planes in the first half of 1917, certain that they had the advantage in performance, armament and usually skill.

Yet though now elatedly flying a Camel I had the feeling that maybe it had come too late. Fighting always against odds on Pups had diminished the zest, and trench-strafing had injured the spirit. When I started the job of fighter pilot, I could, once adjusted to the idea of sudden death, actually enjoy the exhilarating dangers of air combat, of pitting myself against a dog-fight opponent, of diving recklessly on two-seaters, of pluming myself over a bullet that had missed me by an inch. But as I passed through successive weeks and months of risk and strain, I began to realise that some of the fire was beginning to fade out of me.

And maybe that was why I welcomed the thought that I was approaching the time for transfer to Home Establishment. I'd been out in France longer by a month than any other officer in the squadron, for all those who were here before me had been killed or wounded or posted home. Soon I should have done my last patrol in 46 Squadron, but I should be sorry when the time came, for I should not want to leave the newcomers, like the fellows behind me, who had yet to pass through the fiery ordeal.

And those of us who were to pass safely through this strife and bloodshed would be affected by it all the rest of our lives. Our attitude to life itself would always be different from the men who weren't here, the men who ran no risk, who didn't see their comrades slaughtered, in the air, on the ground. Yet I would never have missed it. Vaguely I knew that I was part of a vast experience which I didn't really understand, only that I had joined a valiant company, and although maybe I'd not matched up in achievement with the best, I was there with them. It was my crowded hour of glorious life.

We are down to a thousand feet, and Izel le Hameau aerodrome lies dead ahead. I turn and look behind me. My four pilots are there, dutifully fixed in their places in formation, their propellers whirling, their gaze bent on me. They are awaiting my orders, I am the flight commander, they look to me for leadership, even in the matter of landing. The twilight is too advanced to risk touching down in formation, especially as there is next to no wind, and I wave my left arm, the signal to break up.

Instantly they turn away and circle, waiting for me to alight first. I make a good three-pointer, then as the others follow me down in succession, taxi quickly to 'B' Flight hangar, where the mechanics stand expectantly. Except for them, the tarmac is without life, the other hangars are closed, the long sailcloth curtains are drawn and roped securely. My patrol is the last of the day. The shades of evening are upon us, the stars are twinkling in the frosty, darkening sky. I wonder whether the Huns we attacked are safely down too.

SEVENTEEN

FULL CIRCLE

On a bright April afternoon in 1918 I was standing on the tarmac at Joyce Green aerodrome, near Dartford, where I had command of 'A' Flight in No. 63 Training Squadron, and was discussing a repair job with my flight-sergeant prior to testing a Camel that had been un-serviceable with engine trouble, when another flight-commander, Captain James, about to take off in an Avro with a pupil, Lieutenant Nash, asked if I would join them in a sham fight for ten minutes.

Having recently been busily engaged in real fights in France, my first reaction was to decline, but then remembering my air fighting practices while learning to fly Pups a year before at Portmeadow aerodrome, which had been quite good fun, I was about to agree when some voice within me said *Don't*. I could not explain why, there was no reason behind it, I had no sort of premonition. Just that strong impulse of *Don't*.

I made some excuse, and an instructor, Lieutenant Ward, went up in his Camel instead. A few minutes later, as I was about to climb into my machine, I saw them circling round each other a thousand feet up, about half a mile east of the aerodrome, by the River Thames. Within seconds of my noticing them, still circling, both planes steeply banking, their wings touched, the two craft swung into each other, and became inter-locked. They seemed to cling together as they fell, then they came apart and hurtled down separately to earth. All three occupants were killed.

The crash signalled the fourth dead pilot in the twelve days I had been at Joyce Green, and during the five months I was to serve there, I was to become well accustomed to fatal crashes as well as a plethora of others where the pilot merely went to hospital or was uninjured. The average death rate was one a week, almost all on Camels, and half of them due to collisions. These figures rivalled the mortality at Filton, where I had learned to fly Avros and B.E.s, but there most crashes were the direct consequence of inadequate instruction.

There were several reasons for the numerous accidents at Joyce Green. First for the inexperienced pilot the Camel was the most treacherous machine of all the aeroplanes of the first war. The instructor could explain but could not teach, how to handle a Camel and how to avoid and escape from spins. Even when the two-seater Camel was introduced—and our first did not arrive until early in June—there was a decided limit to what one could demonstrate in aerobatics because the conversion and the weight of a passenger radically altered the Camel's characteristics, and greatly to the worse.

The high rate of casualties to trainee Camel pilots was common to all training schools, with the result that the average youngster, well aware of the machine's wicked reputation, was in trepidation before he even sat in the cockpit. Even when practised flyers showed how easily the Camel could be tamed, its admitted vices still intimidated the novitiate.

But there was a second cogent cause of crashes at Joyce Green, which was that as an aerodrome it was positively the worst for training purposes in Britain. Situated in a wide stretch of marshland that abutted on to the River Thames, and below its mid-tide level, it was a long narrow field between the River Darenth and Joyce Green Lane which was originally an improvised ground for Vickers, whose sheds were at the Dartford end, to test their early prototype aeroplanes.

To use this waterlogged field for testing every now and then was reasonable and to take advantage of it as an emergency landing ground for Home Defence forces was credible, but to employ it as a flying training station was folly, and as a Camel training station was lunacy. A pupil taking off with a choked or failing engine had to choose, according to wind direction, between drowning in the Thames, half a mile wide at this point; or crashing into the Vickers T.N.T. works or hitting one of their several high chimney stacks; or sinking into a vast sewage farm; or killing himself and numerous patients in a large isolation hospital; or being electrocuted in an electrical station with acres of pylons and cables; or trying to turn and get back to the aerodrome.

Unfortunately, many pupils, confronted with disaster in every direction, tried the last course, and span to their deaths. It was my misfortune to witness several of these fatal crashes, not only spins close to the aerodrome, but collisions between Camels during sham fights. One of these I happened to see take place south of Dartford when in the air a quarter of a mile away, giving dual instruction in an Avro. One of the pilots then killed was the South African Lieutenant Van Ryneveld, the younger brother of Colonel Van Ryneveld, at that time commanding the Eleventh Wing of the R.F.C. in France.

Another crash confirmed me in one of the illogical superstitions that I, like most men whose work lay in risky spheres but who found no staff in religion, often turned to. One of my pupils, Lieutenant Williams, in whom I had taken a special interest because he was, like me, a Sherwood Forester, had gained his Wings, and he asked my wife and me to celebrate with him in town. At the Comedy Restaurant, then much in favour with flyers and their ladies, he insisted, despite my half-joking protests, on being third to light a cigarette from a match. Next morning he dived into the Darenth off a spin. I saw it happen, hastily called the Medical Officer, took an Avro and dropped on the other side of the creek, alongside the crash. I helped to pull him out, but he was dead. One should never do these things, for they do one no good, but they have to be tried if there is the slightest hope.

To me it was excessively distressing to see pupils spinning to their death because of the inadequacies of the aerodrome, especially as across the river, in Essex, there were scores of acres of unobstructed level grassland which we flew to for forced landing practice, and which could readily have been made into good aerodromes. One could accept one's friends and comrades being killed in France in combat, even when they had to fight on inferior machines, but for their lives to be thrown away in England on account of the apathetic official attitude of accepting Joyce Green because it happened to be already there, always made me see red.

The defects of the aerodrome were not limited to the surrounding death-traps. It had high dykes on two sides, on which an unwary pupil could catch his undercarriage when either landing or taking off. The landing area was intersected with drainage channels covered with duckboards, the gaps between the battens being nicely calculated to trap the tail skids of taxi-ing planes. A special technique was required to cross the winding duckboards at a good angle, for if the tail skid became wedged the fuselage longerons could easily be twisted and broken, which was a major repair job. Rather than taxi any distance along the aerodrome, it was easier and safer to fly and this we usually did when making for the Mess for lunch.

All the lives lost in the four collisions which occurred at Joyce Green during my time there could have been saved had we been provided with parachutes. During my time in France, as the expansion of the Flying Corps marched with an increasing intensity of air fighting, it became more and more obvious, at any rate to those who had to do the fighting, that many lives could have been saved had the occupants of stricken machines possessed parachutes. A static type, the Calthrop, had been specifically designed for use in aeroplanes, as distinguished from observation balloons, and was successfully employed for dropping spies at night behind the enemy lines in France.

Though far from perfect, as were also most of our aeroplanes, this parachute could have filled the gap temporarily and could have been developed into a free-fall type at little cost compared with the immense funds being poured out on militarily inefficient aeroplanes and faultily designed engines, but the top officers of the R.F.C. and later of the R.A.F. were obstinately opposed even to experiments.[1]

The resistance to introducing parachutes to the battlefield became even stronger when training units were mentioned. So far as take-off crashes were concerned, parachutes would admittedly have been useless, but as I saw at Joyce Green, and as happened at most other

---

[1]This astonishing streak of official perversity, which cost hundreds of airmen their lives, is discussed in my book *No Parachute*, Appendix C.

advanced training stations for fighters, there were many collisions during air fighting practices, and in these, parachutes could always have saved lives.

The casual official attitude to flying casualties during training did not endear me greatly to flying instruction. When posted to Home Establishment from France, I had hoped to go to a Home Defence squadron, but instead had to face the prospect of doing something which, at the receiving end a year previously, I had never greatly esteemed.

When I arrived at Joyce Green after spells of leave and hospital, I had not flown for nearly four months, and I spent my first couple of weeks getting my hand in on Camels. My next hurdle was more tricky, for although I had done over four hundred hours flying, I had never taken up a passenger, other than my early instructors, and now flinched from doing it. Eventually the day came when after turning an Avro inside out to make sure of it, I ventured to take up the commanding officer, Major Crighton, after which my inhibitions left me.

But I could not pretend to be keen on the work of instructing, especially the drudgery of starting pupils off from scratch, and as soon as I got into my stride, I passed most of the *ab initio* training to junior instructors, and confined myself to testing the pupils, checking and confirming their progress, and doing fighting instruction on Camels.

As an instructor I was all too aware of my ignorance, for I had been given no opportunity to learn how to instruct, but with memories of how unhelpful some of my own mentors had been, I tried to be different, especially in allowing the pupils full handling of the dual-control machines. We now had speaking tubes which made instruction in the air far easier. I could boast that none of my advanced pupils had blameable crashes, except in the matter of Camel spins, and to prevent these was something that no instructor at that time seemed to be able to do.

I found myself becoming interested in the work of the pupils, in watching their response, and in feeling duly gratified when they made progress, and especially when they graduated for their wings. Some of them took to flying quickly, others were so dense and hamfisted that it was a waste of effort to struggle with them, and a proportion had to be turned down as hopeless. I had some first-class instructors in 'A' Flight, among them McCrea, Cox, Knocker and Nicholson, and though we worked very hard to try to maintain our assigned output of trained pilots, results were affected by both the aerodrome's crash proneness and the noticeably declining standard of the pupils. One could only suppose that nearly four years of war had had its effect on the quality of our younger manhood.

Of my instructors, Nicholson I remember as a very fine Camel pilot, whose low rolls just about the hangars I never dared to emulate. Knocker arrived after me, straight from hospital after being wounded in France. On his second day, while standing by an Avro on the tarmac, he put his head in the path of a revolving propeller, and by a miracle was not killed, but off he went back to hospital for a time. His father was a horrified spectator of this accident. Of the two other instructors, Cox stayed in the R.A.F. and I met him several times afterwards.

For some three months, I had a flight of a United States aero squadron attached to 'A' Flight for instruction, and the men teamed up quite remarkably well with our personnel in maintenance and other duties. It was extraordinary how quickly and easily they adapted themselves to our ways, and with such goodwill that after a week or so we scarcely differentiated between them and our own men. Almost all of them were eager to fly, and I was never short of passengers when testing Avros or the two-seater Camel.

I had an American private as my passenger when I all but blotted my copy-book on my first flight in the two-seater Camel. When it arrived we gathered around it, for we had never seen one before, but the delivery pilot omitted to mention that the tank held only twenty minutes petrol, most of which he had consumed bringing it to us. I put the American in the instructor's seat and went up immediately, and circled the aerodrome to get the feel of it. In the second circuit, I was halfway across the Thames at 300 feet when the engine spluttered out. Fortunately, though facing north, I had already banked the plane on the curve of the circuit, and was just able to scrape into the aerodrome with the tank completely dry. The mechanic was highly impressed, as he thought I had done it according to plan.

One of the strangest aspects of Joyce Green aerodrome was its position below river level, for at high tide you could stand on the broad dyke, with the Thames swirling a few feet beneath you on one side, and on the other a sunken aerodrome with hangars and aeroplanes some twenty feet or more down. Looking towards the riverside hangars from the landing area when the tide was high, you'd see large ships apparently steaming along on top of the hangars.[1]

Although so ill-sited, Joyce Green had enjoyed a long history in both Home Defence and Flying Training. Among the well-known pilots who had flown there in 63 Squadron were McCudden, who was instructing in mid-1917, and Mannock, who was one of his pupils. McCudden visited Joyce Green during my spell there, and we exchanged reminiscences over the Cambrai show, in which he had added several Huns to his already high score. He commiserated with me at having been employed on ground-strafing, and said he was dead against fighters being wasted on such work. A few days later, on July 9th, he was killed in a flying accident in France, while piloting his S.E.5a to take command of 60 Squadron.

On April 1st, a few days before I arrived at 63 Squadron, an important event had occurred, nothing less than the formation of the Royal Air Force, but I cannot say that this had the slightest impact at Joyce Green, and indeed for most of us the change only began to take effect months later, and then chiefly in the matter of uniforms and ranks. When these innovations came we did not welcome them, for they had been thought up by a Committee strongly biased towards naval practice, with the result that a service which had been

---

[1]Fifty-one years later I stood alongside what was left of the aerodrome and again saw large vessels apparently floating along the top of the dyke. Over the southern end of the old airfield, large model aeroplanes, flown by a group of enthusiasts of the North Kent Nomads Flying Club, skimmed swiftly around me, looping and rolling and steeply banking just as Camels had done half a century before. They gave me a queer sensation of being part of a vision of the past.

predominantly military was given a distinctly nautical image.

Those of us with the army background particularly resented losing ranks such as captain, major and colonel in exchange for flight lieutenant, squadron leader, wing commander and group captain, all distinctly salty, and we also much disliked giving up our rank stars and crowns for sleeve stripes and vertical gilt bars on either side of the cap badge—these last evoking such ridicule that they were soon abandoned.

The first R.A.F. uniform was in khaki in R.N.A.S. style, but this became a light blue (chosen according to rumour by a popular actress) with gold stripes, but again ridicule, aided by the oil and dirt in aeroplanes, forced the adoption of a more practical darker blue with black braid rank stripes. We had to carry not swagger canes but yellowish walking sticks with curved handles, which collectively made an absurd sight on parade. Years later these were abandoned too.

Fortunately, while the war lasted, no pressure was exerted to compel the adoption of these new-fangled notions, and most of us clung to our sentimentally precious regimental tunics and R.F.C. maternity jackets, which we patched with leather until they were worn to tatters. Even when we were eventually forced to adopt the new blue, we still for some years wore breeches and puttees, while officers of squadron leader rank and above sported black field boots.

What every flying man in the new service found difficult to swallow was its label, for the initials R.A.F. stood also for the Royal Aircraft Factory, whose name had accumulated much derision and dislike during the war because it was held chiefly responsible for governmental mass production of death-trap aeroplanes and indifferent engines. Although to aid a proper differentiation the Factory became an Establishment, years were to pass before flying people forgot to wince when R.A.F. was mentioned.

Meanwhile, across the Channel, more important happenings than even the creation of the R.A.F. were in progress, for the German attempt at a breakthrough in March had been held, and the French and British had girded their loins for the counter-attack. In August, the first advances began, and from that time the Germans were on the retreat under continuous and relentless pressure.

In the British March retreat, as in the summer offensive, fighters were employed unsparingly in ground-attack operations, and not un-expectedly the squadrons concerned suffered a high casualty rate. As the advance developed and the intensity of the fighting increased, so fighter losses mounted, and with them the corresponding demand for replacements from home. It came as no surprise to me when, halfway through September, I was warned for overseas, but instead of being sent to 46 Squadron, which I would have chosen had I been asked, I was told that my destination was a squadron yet to be formed, which would be equipped with the new Sopwith Trench Fighter 2, or T.F.2, otherwise, more colourfully, the Salamander.

This was a development of the Snipe, successor to the Camel, and was intended specifically for ground-strafing, the cockpit and fuel tanks being well protected by armour plating. With a 230 h.p. Bent-ley, B.R.2 engine, a pair of Vickers guns and a speed of 125 miles an hour, it sounded a formidable proposition. I had never seen one, but Knocker had inspected one at Brooklands a month earlier, and thought it seemed a heavy and awkward looking machine.

I had much disliked my spell of ground-strafing in France, and was not at first greatly thrilled at the notion of going to a squadron which would do nothing else, but then I realised that I would have to do low work on the Camel or Snipe in any case, and I might as well do it in an airborne tank. So I said good-bye to Joyce Green, where in five months I had done 240 hours flying instruction, an av-erage of two hours every day, but instead of going to wherever the Salamander was forming, I was ordered to do a refresher course at the School of Aerial Fighting at Marske, near Middlesbrough.

Much surprised, I pointed out that first, I had just completed five months as an instructor in air fighting at Joyce Green, having previ-ously done some of the real thing in France, and second, what was the use of an air fighting course to me when I was to pilot a trench-strafing machine that with 650 lb of armour plate hadn't a hope of engaging in air combat?

My argument went unheeded, and I was about to set out for Marske when I was flattened by an acute attack of appendicitis and rushed at once to Sister Agnes's, otherwise King Edward VII's Hospital, then in Grosvenor Crescent. Here I was operated on, and later sent on sick leave.

When I returned to duty, the end of the war was near. By the beginning of November, Turkey had collapsed, on the 3rd Austria surrendered, on the 9th the Kaiser abdicated. I was in London when the news of the signing of the Armistice arrived, and took part in the incredible mafficking that began immediately after the eleventh hour, when church bells pealed from every tower and a joyous madness seized the multitude that rushed to the centre of the capital. A great jubilant crowd assembled outside Buckingham Palace, singing the National Anthem, while King George appeared on the balcony and tried to speak to them.

The first night saw the most frenzied scenes of all, when a seething mass of cheering, singing, rejoicing people crammed all the streets around Piccadilly Circus, from the Ritz through Leicester Square to Trafalgar Square, where groups of soldiers expressed their delight by overturning taxi-cabs and setting them alight. For three days, and most of three nights, the celebrating went on, then the exhausted citizens and troops relaxed and tried to return to normal.

Though it was indeed a memorable experience to join in this extraordinary demonstration, I would have much preferred to be in France. How wonderful it must have been for the lucky ones there to be able to fly along the Lines in safety, knowing that there would be no bursting shells from archie, no bullets cracking past from the Spandaus of an Albatros or Fokker. This was surely the most moving and exalting moment of the war.

Everything that closely followed the armistice seemed an anticlimax. The Salamander posting was cancelled, the squadron was never formed, most of the machines already produced got no further than the acceptance parks, and the type was later abandoned. No. 63 Squadron had moved to Redcar, in Yorkshire, and although I had no wish to follow, I was instead inflicted with a succession of stop-gap postings in the London area—Kenley, Croydon, Fairlop, near Ilford, and London Colney, near Radlett.

All these stations were afflicted with post-armistice apathy, with instructors giving half-hearted flying instruction to carefree pupils, and nothing of note taking place at any of them except Fairlop, previously a training squadron of the R.N.A.S. Here the former ratings became infected with the unrest which had swept through hundreds of thousands of troops, now idle, eager to get back to their jobs before smarter comrades seized them, but frustrated by the, to them, inexplicable bureaucratic delays in demobilisation. Outbreaks of mutiny and near mutiny took place at several army assembly camps, some accompanied by violence. Thus far the R.A.F. had escaped major difficulties, but in late December, with Christmas drawing near, trouble suddenly erupted at Fairlop.

I arrived at the camp one morning at eight o'clock to be told by the sergeant-major that the men had mutinied. They had refused to parade or carry out any work until something was done to hasten the process of demobilisation. The other flight-commander, Captain 'Boy' Bouchier, and I were baffled by a situation so outside our experience, and nothing happened until the C.O. arrived, Major Keith Park.

The position was made clear by the sergeant-major, who emphasised that the men were in a nasty mood. He was told by Park to request them all to assemble in a hangar, where he would attend to their complaint. The men slowly and suspiciously crowded into a hangar, and Park, mounting a box so that all could see him, began to address them very quietly, but without a break, never drawing breath, one word running always to the next. He gave them not a split second's opportunity to interrupt but just went on talking about everything, demobilisation, work, war, peace, jobs, pride, the R.N.A.S., the R.A.F., the price of beer, the wonder of waiting women, anything that came into his head that had even the remotest relevance to the situation.

He spoke in a calm, persuasive and as I quickly realised, monotonous voice, that soon began to have an almost hypnotic effect. Standing behind him, I noticed that after ten minutes the men were showing signs of restlessness, and after twenty minutes all of them were wilting. Park had reached a point when I was half expecting some of the older men to collapse when he stopped on a note of indefinite promise, and left the hangar. Relaxing in relief, the men sheepishly followed and went to their jobs. The mutiny was over.

My one outstanding stop-gap posting before 1918 ended was to attend a course at the South-Eastern Area Flying Instructors' School at Shoreham. I had completed nearly six months as an instructor at an assortment of stations, and there was now almost nobody to instruct, for no more new pilots were wanted, yet here I was at last doing the thing I should have done first, setting out to learn to be a flying instructor.

The S.E.A.F.I.S. was an offshoot of the famed Gosport School of Special Flying, started in 1917 by that notable officer, Colonel R. R. Smith-Barry, which revolutionised flying instruction methods. Shoreham was commanded by Major Dirk Cloete a South African, and my instructors were Captains Hawkins and Vincent. The accuracy of their handling and landing of Pups and Avros was impressive, but even more impressive was the clarity with which I was made aware of my ignorance about flying and instruction.

After 700 hours flying as a pilot, I had thought when I arrived at Shoreham to be a pupil, to learn to fly again, that this was where I came in. But as the course progressed, I realised that I had been flying for nearly two and a half years without knowing how, for I had never formulated in my mind even the first elements of flying or of instruction. And the way in which everything was now explained and demonstrated, the detailed mechanics of piloting and aerobatics and instruction, all this was to me a revelation. And when at the end of the course, I was given an A1 category as flying instructor, I was proud of it. As both pupil and instructor, I felt that I had achieved the veritable Full Circle.

EIGHTEEN
TAILPIECE

Not long before this book was written I paid a summer time visit to the British battlefields of the Western Front of the First World War, most of which I had known in varying degree, from the air and on the ground, during my service in France in 1917.

I began the tour at Ypres, the moated city over which I had so often flown in wartime, and on one special occasion entered. In those days it was a desolation of shell-shattered buildings, but now I walked through a bustling market town which had put aside war, even the last one. I passed the fine rebuilt Cloth Hall and went on to the Menin Gate, where, not for the first time, I stood subdued before the incredible significance of this grim monument, carrying the 55,000 carven names of those who fell in the Salient but of whose bodies no trace was found.

Then came the drive through flourishing farmlands to a few of the largest of the 170 cemeteries that make this region a widespread necropolis, yet one that gives a fitting resting place to the hundreds of thousands of those whose identifiable remains were long ago recovered from the pulverised earth. And as I had found on previous visits, I was humbled at the thought that this legion of the dead had surrendered their lives for no other reason than to preserve Britain and her magnificent heritage.

Working south, I came to the Wytschaete and Messines ridge,

where nineteen giant mines exploded on that unforgettable morning of June 7th, when nearly 500 tons of ammonal blew the crest of the impregnable ridge high into the air. The once raw craters that had sent 10,000 German troops to instant eternity were now attractive, tree-lined lakes, much prized by the local fishermen.

The locality of this patiently planned operation, which for once produced a British casualty list that was miniscule by Passchendaele standards, was of particular interest to me, because I flew over the craters an hour after they had erupted, and also because when, a few days earlier, I had forced landed alongside nearby Dickebusch Lake, I had in a brief visit to the front line unknowingly passed close to the entrance of the most heavily charged of all the mines, at St Eloi.

From Messines I continued south through Ploegsteert Wood and down by La Bassée, Loos and Vimy Ridge, with its magnificent Canadian memorial, to Arras and the Scarpe. Here was the scene of the infamous Bloody April, during which the Royal Flying Corps suffered the heaviest losses in its history, when half-trained youngsters mounted on aeroplanes long due for the scrap-heap were butchered by the dozen by Richtofen and other seasoned pilots flying their efficient Albatroses.

All along the line of battle, and further south, down on the murderous Somme, the chains of cemeteries, those mournful plantations of identical crosses, spoke again of thousands and thousands of lives sacrificed in the service of King and Country. But now, apart from these well-tended acres of hallowed ground, topped by the fluttering Union Jack, the countryside was without trace of war. The sun shone upon the good earth carpeted with bountiful crops, and the light breeze sent ripples along level fields of wheat where once stood men in trenches, behind miles of coiled barbed wire, slaughtering each other across ground pitted by thousand upon thousand of high explosive shells.

From the Somme, I turned north-eastwards towards the terrain of the Battle of Cambrai, which also had special memories for me, for not only did I join in the assault by the tanks with low-flying attacks on enemy positions, but because I was shot down three times in the forefront of the battle, and so saw something of the fighting on the ground. Thus it was that here I at once found myself returning vividly to the past.

Because the Cambrai attack was a brief episode of mobile war, the fighting, after the Hindenburg Defences were crossed, took place in open country until then untouched by operations, and although many villages and farms were damaged by shell-fire, the places I had known were easily recognised. I stood among the farmlands by Anneux where, after my Camel was hit by archie, I had descended behind a fierce struggle in progress less than a mile to the north, to find myself among field guns in action, horse-drawn limbers, stacks of ammunition, first aid posts, infantry reserves moving up, walking wounded coming back, and all the rest of the rearward paraphernalia of battle. But now the fields were smiling, the corn was high, the nearby villages were prosperous, the houses tidy and newly painted.

Between Fontaine and Cantaing I walked across the wide expanse of meadowland where a shell burst had brought my aeroplane down between the German and British lines. Now hundreds of acres of rich crops stretched away eastwards to La Folie Wood, from where enemy machine-gunners had done their best to get me as I ran for my life to the shelter of the sunken road in which my car now stood.

The third spot I searched for and soon found was the gentle knoll south of the Cambrai–Bapaume road below Bourlon Wood, where I had hurriedly descended with a white plume of vaporised petrol streaming from my petrol tank, holed by machine-gun fire from the ground. I landed by a field battery, where I spent twenty-four hours, a thrilled and fascinated spectator of some of the desperate fighting for Bourlon Wood and Fontaine.

It was while waiting for a tender from my squadron to salvage the damaged Camel that I took a walk with one of the gunner officers to Flesquières, where the advance of the tanks had been so disastrously held up on the morning of November 20th. On the way we passed a German two-seater aeroplane shot down a day or two previously. The machine had been wrecked in the crash and souvenir hunters had removed everything detachable, including the cockpit instruments, the machine-guns, and the fabric Iron Crosses. A small mound close by was the grave of the crew. It was not a sight for me to linger at, and we continued on to the south-eastern end of the ridge on which Flesquières stood.

By the high, broken wall that enclosed the wooded grounds of the château, I saw the line of burnt out tanks standing in disarray, caught one by one by a German field battery as they crested the rise six mornings before. Alongside each tank, as also near the battery emplacements by the wall, lay the graves of their crews. This was a setting of desperate valour on the part of both British and German, and one which had always remained compellingly in my memory.

And now, on a summer's day in peacetime, fifty-odd years later, I stood once more at the corner of the château wall and tried to vision the dark shapes of the stricken ironclads sprawling along the top of the slope before me. But it was difficult, for here too the corn was high, covering even the lie of the land, so that no reminder existed of that fatal encounter—save only the château wall, long since rebuilt.

As I had seen everywhere else along the Front, the wounds of war had been healed by nature many years before, but in my memory the burial mounds of the tank crews and of the German gunners, as well as of the two flyers who had fallen a few hundred yards away, still persisted. From them, my thoughts went again to the battlefields I had passed through, where multitudes of the men of my time had been massacred in the remorseless folly of war, hundreds of thousands of them, the cream of our nation, giving up their lives under the simple impulse of patriotism. And among them were many scores of my friends and comrades of the Sherwood Foresters, as well as of the Flying Corps, and especially of my own squadron, the pilots alongside whom I had flown and fought in the skies above.

Here at the corner of the château wall, in the sunshine, by the waving grain, with everything now at peace, I remembered them and was filled with a heavy sense of loneliness. I knew that although I had not been killed, something in me had. Something had gone out of me and was buried, and would always be buried, in a hundred cemeteries, in France and in England, along with the companions of my youth who had died that our country might live.

On the fertile plains of Belgium and France, the greater part of a million British soldiers and airmen consecrated their lives that half century ago. Where we who fought in the air counted our losses by the score, the men in the trenches fell by the ten thousand—and the result was a million dead. This is a figure the human mind cannot grasp, and especially so long after the event. A hundred lives lost in an aeroplane accident conveys a meaning, but to most of us a million corpses has no more significance than a million light-years.

Who today reflects that in the Battle of the Somme alone, where every man was an eager volunteer of 'Kitchener's Army', more British lives were lost than in the whole of the Second World War? Or that in the first day's fighting of any major attack on the Western Front, more men were killed than the Americans lost in eight years fighting in Vietnam?—31,000 at the time these words are written. The average man and woman of today is not interested in such profitless comparisons. Modern life does not want to hear about these inconceivable calamities of the past.

And as I lingered by the château wall, I asked myself, what was it all for? Those holocausts on the ground, and in miniature in the air, that had destroyed the best in our nation—as they had in France, Germany, Italy, Austria, Russia—what had they achieved? What benefit had this war, 'the war to end all wars' conferred on Britain, on the Britain of today?

Fifty years ago, Britain and the British Empire which kept half the globe at peace, the wide dominion that had evolved through the centuries from 'this England' of Shakespeare and Elizabeth I, was a Motherland that men, not only from Britain but from all the Dominions, were proud to fight for and to die for. But today our once mighty Empire lies shattered, our fine heritage has been dissipated, and the greatest World Power of 1914 is reduced to a third-rate state, a cypher in world affairs, a 'toothless bulldog'. We have squandered our resources and our authority, abdicated ingloriously, broken faith with our friends. The ideals of patriotism, honour and duty which inspired us in the past, the achievements of an Empire, which, following in the footsteps of Rome, advanced the well-being of half the world, the beliefs for which a million Britons from throughout the Empire gave their lives, all these have become something to sneer at, even to vilify.

I asked myself, as many others of my generation have done, especially in the past two decades, is the Britain of today in any sense the country which these myriad Britons died to preserve? Was their sacrifice thrown to the winds? Would we, instead of allowing ourselves to be jockeyed unprepared into the arbitrament of a continental war, have been wiser to compromise with the Kaiser's Germany? Would Prussian militarism have been worse to live with than the cruel tyrannies the world has since had to endure?

Had the nations of Europe been persuaded by bold diplomacy to compose their differences before events took charge they would not have embarked on these suicidal courses, and thrown away the leadership of the world. Every nation on earth, however small or backward, could have followed an orderly path of progress. Britain and her Commonwealth, sustained by a million young lives spared, could have retained her strength and unity. In other countries seven million more good lives would have been saved. The monsters of Russian and Chinese communism would not have been born. Hitler and the Nazi war would never have been. The world would not be in ceaseless torment, with scarcely a sunrise without some new act of war and oppression. And we should not all exist as we do today under the constant menace of extermination by nuclear bomb.

At the corner of a field in France, on the ridge at Flesquières, where brave men fought to the death all those years ago, like the million other dead British who fought on the ground and in the air, I asked myself, was their sacrifice worth while? Perhaps the shades of those who are buried in the vast graveyards of France and Belgium, if they could but speak, would know the answer.

INDEX

213